33 MONTHS as a POW in Stalag Luft III

33 MONTHS as a POW in Stalag Luft III

★★★★★★★★★★★★★★★★★★★★★★★

A World War II Airman Tells His Story

★★★★★★★★★★★★★★★★★★★★★★★

Albert P. Clark

Fulcrum Publishing
Golden, Colorado

Library of Congress Cataloging-in-Publication Data
Clark, A. P. (Albert Patton), 1913-
    33 months as a POW in Stalag Luft III : a World War II airman tells his story / Albert P. Clark.
    p. cm.
    ISBN 1-55591-536-1
    1. Clark, A. P. (Albert Patton), 1913- 2. Stalag Luft III. 3. World War, 1939-1945—Prisoners and prisons, German. 4. World War, 1939-1945—Personal narratives, American. 5. Prisoners of war—Germany—Biography. 6. Prisoners of war—United States—Biography. I. Title: Thirty three months as a POW in Stalag Luft III. II. Title.
    D805.5.S745C53 2005
    940.54'7243'092—dc22

                                                                2004030230

Printed in the United States of America
0 9 8 7 6 5 4 3 2

Editorial: Faith Marcovecchio, Haley Groce
Design: Patty Maher
Cover illustration: Copyright © 2003 by Clark Lincoln

Fulcrum Publishing
4690 Table Mountain Dr., Ste. 100
Golden, CO 80403
800-992-2908 • 303-277-1623
www.fulcrumbooks.com

Contents

★ ★ ★

A. P. Clark (center) with Buck Inghram (left) and Ed Tovrea. Courtesy of the Air Force Academy Library

Foreword

★★★

I came to realize that our group was unique. We were survivors of a series of screening and selection processes that were most unusual. First we had volunteered to go to war as aviators. We had been found qualified after a demanding selection process, had graduated from a dangerous flight training program with a high attrition rate, had gone off to war, entered combat, and then survived a traumatic disaster in the air. There was no other way to join this group. We were different. Our experience had left a mark on us that would remain for the rest of our lives.

—Lt. Gen. A. P. Clark, USAF, Ret.

A prisoner at war is an apt description of a twenty-nine-year-old West Point graduate and fighter pilot who was shot down near Ambleteuse, Pas de Calais, France, and captured by the Germans on July 26, 1942. Lt. Col. A. P. Clark, U.S. Army Air Forces, was among the first American airmen to be captured in occupied Europe during World War II. In writing this memoir, Clark has retraced his steps from entering the war as the group executive of the 31st Fighter Group to his operational missions, shoot down, capture, internment, and finally to liberation. His was a path that was to be followed by more than 40,000 downed American airmen who were to survive captivity in German prisoner of war camps.

Now a retired Air Force lieutenant general, Clark has written a memoir of the most horrific time in his life. It is written in an analytical and insightful manner that has been a hallmark of his persona and of his military career.

Imprisoned for thirty-three months, he was first interned at the Luftwaffe interrogation center at Dulag Luft near Ober Ursel, Germany. Following an interrogation period of several weeks, he was moved to Stalag Luft III where he spent the majority of his imprisonment until evacuation under desperate conditions to Stammlager VIIA at Moosburg in Bavaria. It was there that he, along with an estimated 100,000 Allied soldiers and airmen, was liberated by American forces on April 29, 1945.

As a senior ranking officer at Stalag Luft III, the German prisoner of war camp for Allied airmen made famous by the "Great Escape" of World War II, Clark had the opportunity to view aspects of camp organization and covert intelligence operations from a unique perspective. Once branded as the "most dangerous man at Stalag Luft III" by the camp commandant, Clark was deeply involved in myriad activities kept secret from the Germans. He participated in clandestine intelligence operations and in the establishment of covert communications within the camp and with the Allied forces. He created an elaborate escape organization while working tirelessly to distract the Germans by coordinating and protecting numerous escape attempts. His descriptions of camp life and organization, personalities, clandestine operations, forced marches, and liberation are depicted as he encountered them—unvarnished and without hyperbole.

This rich memoir demonstrates that throughout his prison experience, General Clark exhibited a dedication to duty born of military tradition. His inherent tenacity kept him above intimidation and gave him the will to assist the war effort as a prisoner at war.

—Duane J. Reed
Former Archivist
United States Air Force Academy

Preface

Since my time as a POW in Stalag Luft III was largely spent in planning and executing attempts to escape, I now realize that there is a necessary addition to this book. I need to address the following question: was escape considered a duty for American POWs in World War II?

The Geneva Conventions of 1929 make clear that POWs have a right to seek to escape to rejoin their comrades in arms, and the conventions provide for limited punishment for simple escape attempts where weapons or damage to property are not involved. However, I am not aware of any official policies or regulations issued by American authorities on the matter of escape until after the Korean War. All we knew during World War II was "name, rank, and serial number." This was enough to keep me out of trouble as a new prisoner, but if I had not been initially confined with the British POWs, I don't think that I would have felt any pressure to escape except for the natural ones. For the British, it was their government's policy that prisoners of war had a duty to escape.

POWs seek to escape for a variety of reasons: some do it out of boredom, some seek notoriety, others are attracted by the risks, and then there are those who do it because they understand that it is a duty and they face this duty happily. Some Brits had been prisoners since 1939, and their government's policy (that seeking to escape was a duty) was well known and accepted. However, many went no further than to lend a hand to others more inclined to take the risks. American POWs, including me, who sought to escape or to help others do so as a matter of duty rationalized from the British policy and assumed, correctly I think, that doing so must be consistent with the official American viewpoint whether formalized as policy or not. The U.S. Army apparently did issue guidance to combat forces sometime in late 1943 that if captured they were expected to seek to escape, but I was not aware of it.

After the Great Escape, the British Air Ministry sent instructions through secret channels releasing the British prisoners from their duty to escape; the U.S. Army Air Corps passed no such instructions to us, but our enthusiasm for escape dimmed considerably for a period of time. World War II ended without any guidance on this issue reaching American POWs in Germany, if any had ever in fact been sent.

So all considered, I believe, that the answer to the above question is "no." Escape, as a clear statement of American military policy, was not a matter of duty for POWs in World War II.

In the Korean War, while we were fighting a country that had signed off on the Geneva Conventions, our prisoners in their hands were treated as criminals, thus making them technically ineligible for the provisions of the conventions. They were brutally treated and some were forced to confess to crimes against humanity. Largely because of the location and conditions of their confinement, there was little or no escape.

In reaction to the findings from Korean War debriefings, in 1955 the president directed the Department of Defense to assemble a board to recommend corrective action. As a staff officer in Air Force Headquarters, I supported and advised the Air Force member of this board. It produced, and the president approved, the now familiar *Code of Conduct for Members of the Military Services*. This code provides clear guidance to the serviceman on a broad range of subjects, including his conduct should he become a POW. He is told that he should "continue to resist by all means available" and to "make every effort to escape and to help others to escape." The word "duty" is not used. Every serviceman is required to know and understand this code. This guidance, in effect, makes an American POW a prisoner "at war" rather than a prisoner "of war."

The code was tested thoroughly by the war in Southeast Asia, during which practically every kind of POW experience was seen. After the war, the president again directed that the Department of Defense convene a board to reexamine the code and determine its continued relevance as guidance for our servicemen. I was a member of this board, and we interviewed a variety of soldiers, sailors, and airmen and decided that the code was still proper guidance—only one non-substantive word was changed for clarity. This is the situation as it exists today.

Acknowledgments

I owe a great deal of thanks to the following people who, during the last several years, not only helped me to research, assemble, and edit this work but also provided excellent advice and encouragement:

My son, Pat Clark, for editing

Carolyn and Ted Miller, my daughter and son-in-law, for editing

Mary Gannon Walker, my daughter, for editing

Col. Elliott V. Converse, III USAF (Ret.), for editing

Kalynne Holm for enhancing, sizing, and mounting the illustrations

Clark Lincoln, my nephew, for creating the cover design

Trudy Pollok, for identifying and assembling the illustrations

Duane Reed, archivist at the Air Force Academy, for assisting in all aspects of the work

Introduction

★ ★ ★

It is odd how many men who served in one or another of the country's armed forces during World War II have waited half a century before writing of their experiences. It is also sad, for memories have dimmed and details have been forgotten, perhaps diminishing the value of their writing as useful informal history. I am among those who procrastinated for all these years, and I fear that my recollections may suffer the same fate.

I wrote this story because my family and friends urged me to do so. Although not a very glamorous account, to some degree it is unique. Only a relatively small number of the men who went off to fight the war ended up as prisoners and survived that experience. Prisoners of war have attracted considerable public attention in recent years; often they have been viewed as heroes. Some certainly were. But the status of prisoner of war did not automatically make one a hero; after all, it simply meant that you had surrendered to the enemy. For this reason, most former prisoners of war do not consider themselves to have been heroes. I count myself among that group.

For some reason, my brief combat experience has, in my old age, been much on my mind. In the early morning hours while I await the alarm clock's ugly buzz, I find myself reliving again and again the thrilling moments of combat against the Luftwaffe pilots over the Pas de Calais. I review what I did and what I should or should not have done. The calamitous outcome of this brief aerial combat established a benchmark in my life and, for better or worse, certainly changed it.

In retrospect, I'm sure I emerged from my thirty-three months as a prisoner of war a better person. Professional ambition had gotten me into that predicament in the first place, and I had a lot of time to think about my future career while I was imprisoned. After so many long months of captivity my prospects seemed grim indeed, and my former ardor for rapid advancement cooled. I decided that the best approach would be to do my best in whatever assignments came my way. I learned a lot about living in harmony with others under difficult circumstances, and I gained a clearer recognition of the value of teamwork. These were important dividends from my experience.

The friendships I developed during those unpleasant months are among the warmest and most lasting of my life. The wonderful reunions we've enjoyed through the years have served as testimony to the bonding that so many of us have experienced. During the postwar years I remained active in collecting and recording the history of Stalag Luft III, the camp in which I was incarcerated for most of my time as a prisoner. This collection, which is found in the U.S. Air Force Academy Library, has become an important historical resource for the inspiration and motivation of cadets and a rich source of information for the thousands of former prisoners from Stalag Luft III who seek to clarify, refresh, or confirm personal experiences.

CHAPTER 1

Arrival in England

23 June 1942

It was late in the afternoon of a fair but hazy day in June 1942 when I stood on the deck of the SS *Ranpura* as it approached the Firth of Clyde in western Scotland. Spitfires had met us well out to sea and escorted us in. I watched them with keen interest, for we were soon to be equipped with the Spitfire. We were the 31st Pursuit Group, 8th U.S. Army Air Forces, and the first complete American combat unit to arrive in Britain. Part of a fast three-ship convoy, we were fourteen days out of New York. The other passenger ship in the convoy was the SS *Empress of India*, bringing to England the Canadian Essex Scottish Regiment, soon to be decimated in the ill-starred Dieppe Raid. We were escorted by a baby carrier bearing a few ancient Swordfish torpedo aircraft on alert against the German submarines that were taking a heavy toll of Allied shipping in the North Atlantic that summer. We practically slept in our life preservers.

The *Ranpura* crept slowly up the narrow firth and dropped anchor opposite the town of Greenock, Scotland. While the crew was dropping the anchor, the captain directed the operation from the bridge. Three times the obviously inexperienced anchor watch reported to the captain, "She's on bottom, Sir." Each time the captain, with growing irritation, told the seamen, "Let her run full out." The third time his voice echoed back from the surrounding hills. We must have been at the turn of the tide since there was no current, but the captain knew that strong currents were coming, as the tidal range is very large in Britain. As the captain's irritation grew, those of us

1

who were hanging over the rail watching this little drama quietly disappeared. Few of us were fully aware of the pressure our captain had been under dodging German submarines for the past two weeks.

We were very close to the shore on both sides and the bucolic sounds and smells from the farms and villages along the firth wafted to us on the evening breeze. The shouts of children playing and the bleating of sheep gave us a feeling of restored safety. They were a welcome change from the hostile environment of the sea that had been ours for the past two weeks.

One of our young pilots, Lt. Henry Assalin, was the son of an army engineer in Greenock, so he was permitted to go ashore briefly to see his father. Unfortunately, Henry was killed in a flying accident in England later that year. What a pity to lose a promising young man like Henry before he could even get into the war.

Promptly the next morning we were bundled off the ship with all our gear and entrained for the town of Atcham in Shropshire. Upon our arrival, I was invited to join our commanding officer, Col. John R. Hawkins, U.S. Military Academy class of 1924, and several others of the group. We were immediately taken to the Red Lion pub, where Maj. Gen. Carl Spaatz, the commander of the newly formed 8th Air Force, and Brig. Gen. Ira Eaker, commander of the 8th Air Force's Bomber Command, were waiting with several members of their staff to greet us. We startled the townspeople, as we were all dressed in our field uniforms with steel helmets, gas masks, field jackets, heavy boots, and canvas leggings. We awkwardly doffed this gear, stacked it in a corner, and sat down to a pint of stout. I felt a little foolish and embarrassed. There was no visible war going on in the British Isles; everyone looked at us with amusement as our uniforms and gear seemed out of place.

We soon settled in on the nearby Royal Air Force air base, which was to be the home of the group headquarters and the 307th and 308th Squadrons until early August. The 309th Squadron was a tenant on the nearby RAF base at the town of High Ercall. Each squadron was authorized about twenty-five pilots and aircraft and several nonflying officers. About one hundred men with necessary equipment were required for the squadron to operate separately.

We were issued our new Spitfire aircraft and promptly commenced flying. We immediately painted the white stars of the United States on the aircraft, but were quickly ordered to paint them out again. I don't know why this was directed, but higher headquarters may have thought that our presence in England was not yet known to the Germans. It was not long, however, before Lord Haw Haw, who broadcast for the Germans in English all over Europe, welcomed us to the theater on Radio Berlin. The U.S. insignia was back on our aircraft in time for the Dieppe Raid on 19 August. This was the entire group's baptism by fire.

The 31st Pursuit Group had been activated on 1 February 1940 at Selfridge Field, Michigan. It was composed of personnel drawn from the famous 1st Pursuit Group, which had been stationed at Selfridge since World War I. For many years after World War I, the Army Air Corps maintained only three stateside pursuit groups: the 20th at March Field, California, the 8th at Langley Field, Virginia, and the 1st at Selfridge. After the war in Europe started, the U.S. armed forces began a rapid expansion, and the formation of the 31st was the first of many new pursuit groups that would be formed by splitting up existing units. Unfortunately, this practice rapidly

A Spitfire VB with the markings of the 308th Squadron of the 31st Fighter Group in Britain in the summer of 1942. Courtesy of the U.S. Air Force Academy Archives

diluted the experience level of each in the process. By the time the 31st reached England, we only had about seven officers with more than three years' commissioned service. This included the group commander, Col. John Hawkins, the group executive (myself), the three squadron commanders, and several nonflying staff officers.

I found that the Spitfire was easy to fly, and the more experienced pilots among us were soon eager to see action. Our less experienced pilots, many of whom had joined the group right out of flying school only a few months before we left the States, were having problems. The only high-performance aircraft they'd flown was the P-39, which was configured with a nose wheel. The Spit was what we called a tail-dragger; it taxied with its nose high in the air and required great care to avoid taxi accidents. Like British bikes, the brakes were operated by hand, which further complicated our transition.

We experienced many accidents during the first two months. I loaned my aircraft to Capt. Frank Hill one day, and he was almost killed when an English pilot landed on top of him just as Frank touched down leading a flight of four aircraft. Neither pilot was hurt, but both aircraft were totally destroyed. I rushed out to the crash site and found Frank standing in the back of an ambulance. He looked at me in embarrassment and said, "I'm sorry I pranged your aircraft, Sir." I let him know it was not his fault.

The accident was caused by the differences between our fighter landing pattern and the pattern the British used. We brought a formation of aircraft in to land with a long, slow, straight-in approach to the landing. The Brits, on the other hand, approached the runway at about 1,500 feet and then made a tight descending turn to the landing spot. Thus a British pilot might easily make his approach without seeing the landing American formation. We soon adopted the British pattern.

One day I was practicing landings. There was one other aircraft in the pattern and I lost sight of him while I was taxiing back for another takeoff. He had run out of gas on final approach and crashed. This was our first fatality. Another pilot was lost attempting a slow roll over the runway, and a third crashed after he fell out of formation at high altitude, probably from hypoxia. In the first three weeks of July, the group destroyed or seriously damaged twenty-one of our new aircraft in flying or taxiing accidents.

Our mail was very uncertain. Procedures for delivery had not been well established in the new European theater, and they were further complicated by the security of our location. I had written a number of letters home but had only received one from my wife, Carolyn. I would not hear from her again for seven months. By this time she and the kids were back in San Antonio living with her father and mother, Col. Arthur and Elizabeth Wilbourn. He was on the staff of the Commander 8th Corps Area and, fortunately, was living in one of the spacious old quarters on the staff post at Fort Sam Houston. Carolyn's sister, Elizabeth, was also living there with her new baby. Elizabeth's husband, John Erickson, also in the Air Corps, was serving overseas in a location unknown to any of us at that time. I missed my family terribly. I had seen so little of them in the hectic past two years.

My wife, Carolyn, and our children, Pat, little Mary, and Carolyn. Photo taken in 1943.

Meanwhile, we rapidly adjusted to British ways and continued the training of our young pilots so that we could consider our group combat ready. We were all issued bikes, and they were our only means of getting around the base. Darkness did not come until eleven o'clock, and in the evening we would sometimes pedal down to a local pub and have a pint. We were on the British ration—lamb, Brussels sprouts, and potatoes—much to our disgust. The lamb came from New Zealand and often arrived in what we considered an inedible condition. The refrigerated warehouses along the Thames had been destroyed in the Blitz, so the lamb had to be moved up-country very quickly and sometimes it didn't make it before it had gone bad. When our cooks threw out the rotten meat and went back for a reissue, they were told, "That's it, governor, scrape it off and cook it!"

For the next several weeks we received lots of attention from distinguished British RAF and American Air Force visitors who were anxious to assess our capabilities and get us into the war. There was strong political pressure from home to get us into action on the Fourth of July. This was manifestly impossible, as we had a lot of training to accomplish with our new aircraft before we could be considered combat ready.

Eventually Major Kagelman, who had recently arrived in Shropshire with some of the personnel of his 15th Light Bomb Group, was ordered to participate with six of his crews in a twelve-aircraft low-level attack on German air bases in Holland on 4 July 1942. A British officer led the attack, and British lend-lease Maryland aircraft were used. Little damage was done, but three aircraft were lost. The only survivor from these three aircraft was an American named Marshall Draper. He thus became the first U.S. Army Air Forces POW in Germany. As for Major Kagelman, his aircraft actually hit the ground after being struck by flak, then bounced back in the air, and Kagelman miraculously flew it home. Overall the mission accomplished little, losses were high, and the helter-skelter way the mission was put together demonstrated that putting political pressure on the folks facing combat tends to cause mistakes.

Things were going rather badly at this time for the British. Singapore had fallen, the cruisers *Repulse* and *Renown* had been sunk off Indochina by Japanese air attacks, Rommel was threatening to take Egypt, and Malta was under heavy air attack. The loss of the two major warships by air bombardment alone convinced all the world's navies that major ships need air cover to survive in dangerous waters. The British Bomber Command had just started the 1,000 bomber night raids on Germany with an attack on Cologne on the night of 30 May. RAF Fighter Command was near the end of a two-year-long unsuccessful effort to assist the Russians by drawing off German fighter forces from the eastern front. This was an aggressive effort involving continuous, strong incursions over the Continent, but losses had been disproportionately high.

At the end of the first week in July, Colonel Hawkins decided that it was time for our three squadron commanders and their deputies to go down and fly with the British in 11 Group. They sorely needed to get some combat experience. Maj. Marvin McNickle was the commander of the 307th and his deputy was Capt. Pat Davis. Maj. Fred Dean commanded the 308th and his deputy was Capt. Del Avery. Capt. Harry Thyng commanded the 309th and his deputy was Salty Chambers. All of them were well qualified and eager to get into it.

This development presented me with a dilemma: I really wanted to go, too. I was ambitious and anxious to gain the combat experience that was the prime requirement for me and all my peers in order for us to advance. I had observed that, since the Battle of Britain, British fighter operations demanded very active flying by the wing commanders. They were the equivalent of our group commanders, and many combat missions flown over the Continent since the Battle of Britain had been large formations led by wing commanders. All were young, in their twenties or early thirties, and most were graduates of the Battle of Britain. They had great prestige and were relieved of the burdens of station administration and logistics by older officers of equal or higher rank. This enabled them to devote all of their attention to the business of fighter tactics and leadership. Our commanding officer, Colonel Hawkins, on the other hand, was more than forty and well beyond the age for active combat flying as it was being conducted from England at that time. I was twenty-nine and very restless to go out and get some combat experience. Understandably, Colonel Hawkins was not enthusiastic about letting me go: as his executive officer and a lieutenant colonel, I was his second in command and we were very busy adjusting to British procedures and training our new pilots. Reluctantly, he released me, and I was very grateful.

CHAPTER 2

Tangmere

13 to 26 July 1942

O n about 13 July, I flew down to Merston Airfield along with Marv McNickle, Fred Dean, Harry Thyng, and their deputies. Our formation of eight aircraft was led by an RAF pilot who had been helping us at Atcham. We were not yet trusted by the Brits to fly into a potential combat zone unattended. Merston was a grass field a few miles southeast of the town of Chichester in West Sussex. The spire of the beautiful old cathedral dominated the horizon and was a useful landmark to help us find our rather obscure little field. Merston, along with West Hampnett and several other small nearby fields, was a satellite of RAF Tangmere, an old base that had been badly damaged in the Blitz and was no longer deemed safe for a concentration of operational aircraft.

When we taxied into the line we were met by Canadian airmen—fitters and riggers, as they are designated in the British service. Both are skilled mechanics and keep the aircraft in flyable condition; the fitter looks after the engine and related parts and the rigger looks after the rest of the aircraft, especially its primary flight surfaces and controls. When they realized we were Americans, they welcomed us with great enthusiasm and voiced their unhappiness with the perception that they were being oversupervised by the Brits. The Tangmere Wing was composed of two British and one Canadian squadron: 129, 131, and 412, respectively. We were assigned to train with several different squadrons. I was assigned to 412 commanded by Squadron Leader R. C. Weston, RAF. Although the Canadians had been in England for more than a year, they were still being led by Brits. Flight Lt. John Gillespie Magee, the young American author of the famous poem "High Flight," had flown with squadron 412. He had been killed in an aircraft accident during the previous winter.

After I was assigned to Yellow Section under Flight Lt. Fred Green, RCAF, I spent most of my time at the alert hut. Our squadron alert hut was located on the edge of the flying field and the in-commission aircraft were lined up on the edge of the field very close to it. We spent our duty time there when not flying— studying, planning missions, and briefing and debriefing pilots. It was the heart to the squadron-level operation. For transportation I was dependent on the squadron lorry, so I didn't get around much. The other members of our group were billeted with the squadron pilots at a comfortable country home called Abbeylands. Because of my rank, which was the equivalent of the Tangmere wing commander flying, I was billeted with the more-senior staff officers in a

Six of the seven pilots from the 31st Fighter Group who were sent down to fly with the RAF Tangmere Wing to gain combat experience. From left to right: Capt. Harry Thyng, Lt. Del Avery, Maj. Marvin McNickle, Capt. Pat Davis, Maj. Fred Dean, and Lt. Salty Chambers. This photograph was taken for publicity purposes in the United States one day after I, the missing member of the group, was shot down. Courtesy of the U.S. Air Force Academy Archives

lovely country estate known as Shopwycke House. While I was comfortable enough, I was isolated from the valuable off-duty company of those with whom I was flying and learning about air fighting. The station commander, Group Captain Appleton, was an older man well beyond the age to be considered eligible for fighter combat flying. Our wing commander flying was named Pedley. I seldom saw him, and I don't recall that he made any effort to help me learn the trade. His carefully groomed and waxed Spit had the Johnnie Walker Scotch whiskey logo painted on its nose, since it had been financed by the distillery. The Brits had a fund-raising program that permitted private organizations to fund a Spit and have it carry their logo.

After about a week of general orientation and training, we were scheduled on ship patrols over the Channel to protect British coastal shipping convoys. Ships were frequently attacked as they passed through the narrows between Dover and Cape Gris-Nez, and the RAF had the onerous task of protecting them. On one of these missions, Harry Thyng, the aggressive squadron commander of our 309th Squadron and a member of our little group of neophytes, got a crack at a German JU-88 and claimed a "damaged." A pilot can claim a damaged enemy aircraft when he or another pilot sees visible signs of damage from gun or rocket fire, such as trailing smoke or fire, shedding pieces of aircraft, and so forth.

We all spent time in the operations center during sweeps over the Continent and became familiar with the tactics and the emergency procedures for recovering downed pilots. Radar was skillfully employed to alert our formations of airborne German aircraft. The British radar was a critically important element in producing a successful mission over the area of our French sweeps. It could identify hostile aircraft as far as sixty miles in from the French coast and warn friendly aircraft of their location.

The Germans had introduced a new fighter aircraft into their formations along the Channel coast in late 1941: the Focke-Wulf (FW) 190. I remember reading in the British magazine *The Aeroplane* that an FW-190 had been captured in June 1942. It landed by mistake in the south of England due to bad weather. Results of the inevitable comparative tests confirming the superiority of the FW-190 over the Spit VB had not yet filtered down to us. These two aircraft were similarly armed, but the FW-190 was proven to be forty-four miles per hour faster than the Spit and had a superior roll rate, which would enable it to disengage by a split-S faster than the Spit. The Spit was only superior in its turn rate.

In the spring of 1942 the Germans had initiated a program of hit-and-run raids along the English Channel coast. (There had been very little aggressive German air activity over the south of England since the Blitz.) These raids, carried out by FW-190s, were more of a nuisance then a serious threat, but they were a matter of considerable interest to us. Hard-to-catch single aircraft, or a pair, would come over late in the evening at very low altitude underneath the radar coverage, drop one bomb, and be gone as quickly as they arrived. We participated in several attempts to ambush these flights without success. They were seen once, but in the tail chase they rapidly pulled away from us, clearly demonstrating their speed advantage. No one in my section ever saw them, but we were told that they were going so fast and so close to the water that they left a wake like a speedboat. I recall how keenly disappointed I was that I still had not even seen an enemy aircraft.

I was very poorly informed on the order of battle of the British and German fighter forces facing each other across the Channel and their relative success. If I had known then what I know now, I would have been considerably sobered. The Luftwaffe was deployed to defend against intrusions anywhere along the occupied western coast of Europe, but it was the elite Jagdgeschwader 26, with about 200 FW-190s, that held the position between the Cherbourg Peninsula and Holland. This was the main area over which the air fighting was now occurring.

The Geschwader (wing) commander of Jagdgeschwader 26, Maj. Gerhard Schöpfel, and his three Gruppe commanders, Seifert, with his squadrons deployed around Saint-Omer, twenty-three miles east of Boulogne; Muencheberg, with his squadrons deployed around Abbéville, sixteen miles east of the Somme estuary; and Prille, with his squadrons deployed north of Calais, were all veterans of the Battle of Britain. They all had impressive records of victories in action against the RAF. Muencheberg, for example, had eighty-one victories as of June 1942. As a matter of policy, the Luftwaffe was placing its best pilots in the west. In the summer of 1942 these forces reached a peak of effectiveness soon lost and never achieved again.

By the end of 1941, Air Vice Marshall Sholto Douglas, commander of RAF Fighter Command, had one hundred fighter squadrons at his disposal. This was a new peak in strength, but the level of training left a lot to be desired. Losses during the last six months of 1941 compelled the War Cabinet to order a more defensive strategy. The Luftwaffe had badly disrupted the RAF daylight operations over the Continent during that period. Between June and the end of December, the RAF reported the loss of 411 fighters over the Continent and the Channel. The comparable German losses for this same period were much lower. In all of 1941, JG26 reported the loss of only forty-seven pilots killed in combat, seventeen in accidents, and three as POWs. I found these statistics in Donald Caldwell's fine book, *JG 26.*

Fighter Command continued the same aggressive pattern of operations into 1942, escorting light bombers (Circuses) and conducting pure fighter sweeps (Rodeos), but tactics were sharpened. Rendezvous were carefully timed, and approaches to the coast were made in radio silence and at very low altitude to stay under the German radar for as long as possible. A rapid climb to altitude was then made to avoid coastal flak. These missions often were able to penetrate before German fighter formations could gain a position above them. British radar was able to give RAF formations timely information about the position and general strength of enemy formations up to fifty or sixty miles in from the Channel coast. The Germans, on the other hand, were often ready for these incursions through signal intelligence, and if British bombers were escorted, the Luftwaffe would attack these formations in strength. If they determined that the RAF was mounting a purely fighter sweep, they would sometimes decline to challenge and not launch their fighters at all.

An unfavorable balance of losses had continued to mount in 1942. In March, RAF Fighter Command lost thirty-two Spitfires with pilots. JG26 lost five pilots. In April, the RAF lost 103 Spitfires and one Hurricane with a group captain and two wing leaders. The Germans lost twelve JAG fighters in combat and five in accidents. British losses on 1 and 2 June were sixteen Spits and fourteen pilots. Caldwell notes in *JG 26* that these losses caused Air Vice Marshall Douglas to report to his superiors, " . . . there is no doubt in my mind or that of my fighter pilots that the FW-190 is the best all-around fighter in the world today."

To continue this unhappy trend, I learned after the war that on 30 July, three days after I was shot down, a Circus including six Boston light bombers heavily escorted by Spit VBs and some of the new Spit IXs made an attack on Abbéville. They lost ten Spit VBs and pilots. JG26 lost one FW-190 and pilot. During the famous but disastrous Dieppe Raid on 19 August, the RAF admitted losses of 106 aircraft and the Germans lost forty-eight, of which twenty were fighters. Again from Caldwell's *JG 26*, the chief inspector of the general staff, Gen. Allan Brook, is reported to have summarized that operation as follows: "This bloody affair, though productive of many valuable lessons, ended the summer's attempt to draw off planes from Russia by trailing Fighter Command's coat over northern France. A gesture that has cost Britain nearly 1,000 pilots and aircraft."

The significance of this unhappy situation to me and the other six American neophytes is obvious. We had been in England for about a month, and each of us had flown the Spitfire for about twenty or thirty hours. As far as I know, none of us had fired his guns except into the sea to be sure they were working. We were about to tangle with the elite of the Luftwaffe fighter forces on their home ground after about two weeks of hasty orientation. We, of course, knew nothing of the odds, and if we had, we would not have cared. We were eager to get into it. But a sense of haste and pressure clearly hung over our introduction to combat, and it stemmed from the very top in Washington.

On about 23 or 24 July, we started flying in a squadron formation and practiced breaking, in other words making an abrupt hard turn of the entire formation in response to an attack from the rear. I had a feeling we would soon be going on a sweep over the Continent. The next day I learned that my aircraft had gone down for repairs, and Group Captain Appleton told me over cocktails that it had popped some rivets in the tail section. He said that when landing on rough fields such as ours, one must avoid holding the tail down hard, as the Spit had a weakness in its tail bulkhead. I would like to have known this sooner, but there were lots of things we hadn't yet learned about our new aircraft and air fighting.

A replacement aircraft was immediately flown down from Atcham and the big white stars on the wings were replaced by RAF roundels; the letters on the sides of the fuselage were hastily changed from the 309th Squadron letters (WZB) to the Canadian Squadron letters (VZG). I was not happy about the loss of my aircraft. We all knew that when one gets a borrowed aircraft from a unit not your own, one never gets the best one. The serial number of my aircraft was EN921 and that of my replacement was EN964. On Saturday afternoon, 25 July, I was told that the next day we would be participating in a sweep over the Continent.

CHAPTER 3

Off for a Rodeo

26 July 1942

After breakfast I was picked up by the squadron lorry and taken to the alert hut. No one was there, and it became clear that all of the wing pilots were attending a briefing about which I had not been informed—this was one of the several disadvantages of my isolated billeting arrangement. As soon as all of the pilots arrived, we hurriedly donned our gear and I was given a hasty briefing by my section leader, Fred Green. As I remember it, he said we were going to make a sweep over Abbéville. We would proceed with radio silence, at minimum altitude, using 1,800 RPM to save gas, until we were close to the French coast. I was to stick close to Green throughout the mission. That was all I knew when we went out to start engines. I had no time to express my anger and indignation at the failure by Green and Squadron Leader Weston to arrange for me to get to the briefing. They had just forgotton about me. We took off in pairs at 1235 hours (double daylight saving time), formed up, and took up a course of about 115 degrees. On this heading, France was about ninety miles away, mostly over water. We ingressed so low that we picked up salt spray on our windshields.

I have since learned that Abbéville is about eighteen miles in from the French coast, behind the Somme River estuary. Its airdrome, Ducrat, was the main base of the 2nd Gruppe of the 26th Jagdgeschwader. We were part of a larger operation with the Biggin Hill Wing (based just southeast of London) attacking Saint-Omer. Saint-Omer's airdrome, Fort Rouge, was thirty miles due east of Boulogne and was the main base for the 1st Gruppe of JG26, which was equipped similarly to the 2nd Gruppe. The Northolt Wing (based just northwest of London) swept the coast of the Pas de Calais in the area of our operation from Le Touquet north to Gravelines. Both of these wings launched at the same time as the Tangmere Wing and used the same approach technique: staying under the German defense radar for as long as possible to achieve surprise. Two spotter aircraft, also Spitfires, were launched at 1330 hours to cover the withdrawal phase of the operation in case any aircraft went down in the Channel. Both these wings and the spotter aircraft saw action and took casualties northwest of Calais.

About ten miles off the French coast our formation began a hard climb, crossing the coast at 10,000 feet and arriving over Abbéville at 10,000 to 12,000 feet. The squadrons were echeloned in height in very tight formation with 412 the bottom squadron.

On the way in, after we knew we were clearly visible to German radar, Wing Leader Pedley, flying with 131 (the high squadron), called 11 Group Control and asked for the "form." He was asking for information on any airborne German aircraft. I did not hear the reply, but I believe control would have reported none, or at least none above us. I believe we achieved tactical surprise, for the flak was heavy over Abbéville and aircraft were observed scrambling to the southwest from Ducrat's only runway.

I was completely surprised when Green suddenly took his section out of the squadron formation in a dive down to the airfield. There, I could see aircraft taking off in pairs. Green and I quickly closed on two just as they became airborne, and he fired at the wingman as they commenced a hard right turn. Green broke off quickly to the left, and since I observed no sign of hits, I also fired a burst at the same aircraft and quickly broke off to follow Green. I don't believe either of us scored a strike on this aircraft.

As I hurried to catch up with Green, he called and said, "Through the gate!" which meant to apply full emergency power as we headed back toward the coast right on the deck—so low that we were under German radar. At this point I was excited and thrilled at having had such an easy shot at the enemy. Naively, I figured that there was more we would accomplish now that we were down there and had come all that way. I called to Green and said, "Let's find something else to shoot up!" Green responded quickly with, "No, let's get the hell out of here!" and I followed him as we raced for the sea on what I assumed was our return heading to England. If I'd had the benefit of the briefing, I would have known that our quick exit from the area was a prerequisite for survival.

The Germans must have quickly directed their aircraft, already airborne, in our direction. Since the war I have learned that some twelve to fifteen airborne FW-190s were observed before our attack on the airfield. I was unable to keep up with Green, although I was going as fast as my aircraft would go. I now realize that I should have requested Green to ease up a little, but I knew that he could see me, and I figured he must know that I had fallen more than a hundred yards behind him.

It wasn't long before I saw four FW-190s closing on me at my six o'clock. I don't remember reporting this to Green, but if I didn't, I should have, for I was soon under fire and a big hole suddenly appeared in my left wing. I knew that if I sat there I would be quickly shot down, so I called Green and said, "I'm breaking left now," and I pulled a hard climbing turn. Green did not follow. I heard no response from him, and I have never seen him since. From then on I was entirely on my own.

I'd planned to execute a 360-degree hard turn and then try to resume my race to the sea. I hadn't completed ninety degrees of my turn, however, before I exchanged fire with a single aircraft in a head-on pass. I continued my turn and, before I completed it, I exchanged fire in another head-on pass with a single aircraft. As we passed each other, wing tip to wing tip, I glimpsed the muzzle flashes from the nose of his aircraft. I then dove down to the deck and sped out to sea. I could see four aircraft chasing me, but they appeared to be holding some distance in trail, possibly to give the coastal flak a chance to fire at me. As I crossed the shoreline, I was fired on by flak and could see the splashes from their fire in the water on both sides of me.

The four FW-190s were closing to finish me off, and I could see their tracers going by. I realized I needed to do something pretty damn quick. Using the only advantage that my aircraft had over theirs—tight turns—I pulled up into a hard loop. To my surprise, when I came out of the loop in a dive to sea level, I had four enemy aircraft trapped right in front of me. I was closing on them fast with the added speed of my dive, but before I reached firing range, they spotted me. Two broke right and two broke left. I closed on the two turning right and fired on the closest, but after a short burst my guns ceased. I was either out of ammunition or my guns had jammed. I quickly broke off again and continued out to sea just off the water. I didn't wait to see if I'd hit the aircraft.

Apparently, the Germans had had enough, as I saw no further aircraft, and I concentrated on heading for England just above the water as fast I could go. After only a few minutes, however, my engine began running rough. Checking my instruments, I noted that my engine coolant temperature gauge was approaching the highest possible reading. What a revolting development, just as it was beginning to look like I might make it home! The Merlin engine didn't run very long after the coolant liquid was gone, and one shot in the radiator or its related plumbing was all it took.

I was a long way from England, and the prospect of a bail out or a ditching was dismal. The Spitfire had a notorious reputation for doing a bad job of ditching. When it hit the water, it tended to be pulled under abruptly by the radiator, which was located under the right wing, and then it headed for the bottom. Just a few days before, Wing Comdr. Paddy Finucane, a distinguished fighter ace, had had to ditch. He had apparently been unhurt, but he never got out of his aircraft. The news of Finucane's loss made me decide that if my engine froze or caught fire over water, I would bail out.

I zoomed up to about 10,000 feet and went through the bail-out drill. Thank God no further enemy aircraft were nearby, as I was

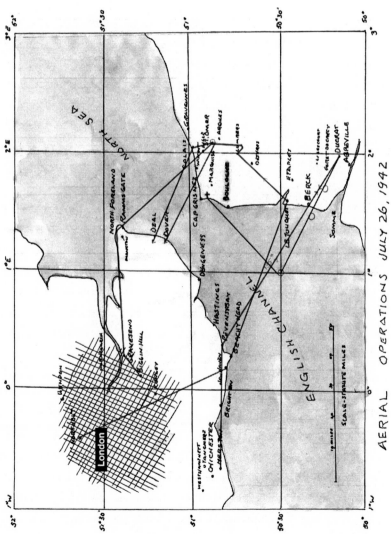

A map of the primary area of operations between RAF fighter wings and Luftwaffe jagdgeschwaders during the summer of 1942. It shows the routes of flight of RAF wings on 26 July 1942. Map by A. P. Clark

completely preoccupied with initiating a Mayday call; switching on my "pip-squeak" tracking transmitter; doffing my helmet, goggles, and oxygen mask; and jettisoning the cockpit canopy. When I pulled the emergency lanyard on the canopy, however, it broke off in my hand; the canopy came loose but did not fall free. I then tried to open it in the normal way, by sliding it back on its track, but it didn't budge. I was now as close to panic as I'd ever been.

To avoid stalling I was forced to descend, and soon I found myself back at sea level, expecting to hit the water at any moment. While my engine sputtered, I desperately looked for land, as a wheels-up crash landing on terra firma was my only hope of survival. A successful ditching with the hatch jammed shut would mean that I would go down with the aircraft. Ditching was bad enough under any circumstances, but trapped in the cockpit, I had no chance of making it out alive in the water. I was badly disoriented but saw land low on the horizon in a direction that I felt was north. In the Spit the compass is on the floor of the cockpit, but since I had braced my feet up against the instrument panel to ease the shock in case I hit the water, I couldn't see the compass. I sputtered in the direction of the land, hoping it would be England. I was going very slowly and was very close to the water. If the Germans had seen me, I would have been a sitting duck.

There was little wave action and I was not more than five feet above the water as I approached the shoreline. I was completely preoccupied with trying to stay airborne, yet I recall that the land appeared flat and treeless with a very shallow bank above a narrow beach and fields out beyond. I didn't know whether I was approaching the southeast coast of England or the west coast of France. They come very close together between Dover and Cape Gris-Nez.

When I reached the shoreline, I noticed a lighthouse off to my left up the coast about a mile. It later turned out to be the Cape Gris-Nez light, and I had made my landfall some thirty miles north of where I was engaged in combat. I lifted the aircraft up over the shallow bank and prepared to land immediately straight ahead in an open field. Ironically, as I pulled up my canopy broke free and disappeared. But I was fully committed to landing, and only later did I consider the options that had suddenly become available to me. I could have turned back out to sea and ditched or tried to reach England, which, unknown to me then, was only about eighteen miles away. In fact I was hoping that this was England and that I was "home and dry," as the Swedes say.

My airspeed indicator was frozen on 320 mph. Apparently the system had been shot out by the cannon shell that tore the big hole in my left wing. As I prepared to land, it became apparent that I had too much airspeed, and up ahead I saw a rock wall lying in my path. If I had hit that wall, it would have been curtains, but fortunately I had enough airspeed left to lift the aircraft over the wall and land in the next field, wheels up. My aircraft hit hard and swung abruptly to the right, dragging on the radiator below the right wing. The edge of the windscreen gave me a hard crack on the top of my head. I was bareheaded but still strapped in, so I wasn't seriously hurt.

One of several photographs of my aircraft taken by the Germans shortly after I crash-landed. They were among a large collection of official German photographs acquired by a Frenchman after the war. They eventually came into the hands of Steve Martin, a Canadian war buff who researched the Canadian war records and discovered that this was my aircraft. He found me and sent me the photos in 1999. The feelings I experienced when I saw them are hard to describe.

I climbed out immediately and stood beside my battered Spit, catching my breath. The engine was spurting very hot coolant from the left side in a steady stream. As I looked around to see where I was and observe any sign of activity, a yellow-nosed FW-190 suddenly

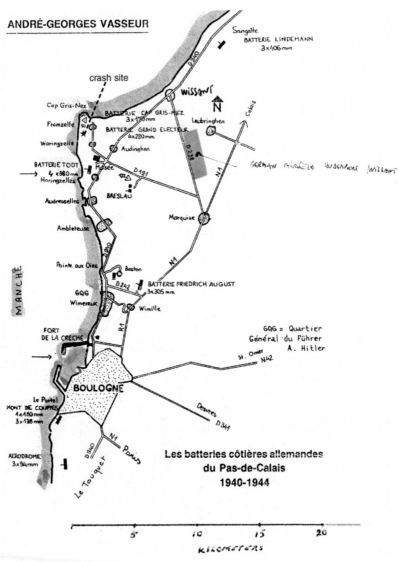

ANDRÉ-GEORGES VASSEUR

crash site

Les batteries côtières allemandes
du Pas-de-Calais
1940-1944

GQG = Quartier
Général du Führer
A. Hitler

Map of the German artillery batteries facing the English Channel from the Pas de Calais during the war. I landed near one of these guns outside of Framzelle. Sketch provided by Andre-Georges Vasseur. The source was probably French wartime intelligence.

buzzed me. My heart sank, for I knew immediately that I must be in France. I looked around for cover, but I was in the middle of a very large field. Armed men wearing white uniform coats were quickly approaching me from two directions. This was it. My whole world came crashing down.

The FW-190 disappeared as the German soldiers arrived and began to lead me toward a hut in the woods, which appeared to be the command post for a flak unit. On the east edge of the field was a huge installation under camouflage netting. The flak unit appeared to be guarding it, since the soldiers had come from gun installations in the nearby woods. While I was being escorted across the field, a single Spitfire made a slow turn over us at about 2,000 feet. It drew fire from the flak guns before disappearing out to sea. I had the feeling that this aircraft had been sent to check out my situation. The air/sea rescue people may have been tracking my flight through my little radio beacon.

A senior noncommissioned officer dressed my cut head. Shortly thereafter, a car arrived and I was driven under guard to what I later learned was the *hôtel de ville* (city hall) of the town of Marquise, about fifteen minutes from my point of capture. I had been handled quite properly and without any hassle or excitement. My captors acted as if they did this kind of thing every day. When I recall that this area had seen intense aerial combat between British and German aircraft since September 1939, especially during and since the Battle of Britain, I realize that one more downed British aircraft was not at all unusual.

I returned to France in 1976 and found the field in which I crash-landed. A huge concrete ruin was still in place there, and I have since learned that it was the site of one of the big 380-mm. coastal batteries that were used against British ships transiting the Channel. Thus the soldiers who captured me were probably German army artillerymen.

At the city hall I was escorted to a small second-floor office where an officer took my name, rank, and serial number; relieved me of my watch, West Point ring, dog tags, and escape packet; and placed them in an envelope. I noticed that my parachute, helmet, goggles, and oxygen mask were on the floor in a corner of his office. He then asked me to follow him, and we went back outside. As I descended the steps of this old stone office building, which faced a small square, I looked up and saw that all of the windows of the French houses across the square were filled with the townsfolk quietly watching. They apparently had learned that the Americans had finally begun to arrive in France. Neither I nor they would have believed that it would be another two long years before we would arrive on French soil in force.

I was escorted under guard around the corner to a house facing the narrow street. It was an officers' mess. I was placed in a reading room alone with the doors either locked or guarded. After being quietly warned that if I attempted to escape I would be shot, I was held there for the rest of the afternoon with nothing to do but consider my predicament.

I felt terribly embarrassed for letting down my comrades. Here I was, the second most senior and experienced pilot in our group, responsible for the training of our young pilots, and I had become the first battle casualty. I was quite sure that this unhappy day marked the end of my career in the service. I was also angry. I felt that I had been left to my fate by my section leader, Flight Lieutenant Green, who had first sped west so fast that I could not keep up with him even at emergency full power, and then had failed to cover me when I called for an emergency break after being fired upon by overtaking enemy aircraft. All fighter pilots knew that if you fell behind you were asking to be shot down, so we absolutely depended on mutual support.

After the war I learned that the British commander of 412th Squadron was replaced two days after that mission. In retrospect I sensed no enthusiasm on the part of any of the senior British personnel with whom I was in daily contact to help me learn the combat business. They were more aloof than friendly and may have been unable to accept an officer of my rank with no combat experience. I had thought that they would eagerly welcome our assistance in fighting the war and break their backs to help us get qualified for the fight. I did not know then that I would have almost three years as a prisoner to mull this point over and feel bitter about it, if I chose to.

When dinnertime finally arrived, I was escorted to the dining room where some fifteen officers in green uniforms were assembled around a large table that filled the room. We were seated and served a cold plate of bread, sausage, and cheeses, probably a typical Sunday night supper. Before I had finished my meal, a fairly senior German officer arrived and went around the table, meticulously saluting and shaking hands with each of us. He was dressed in a blue uniform and was well decorated. After a few words I was asked to accompany him. I believe he may have been Maj. Gerhard Schöpfel, the commander of JG26 and the elite Luftwaffe fighter wing who faced Britain in the Pas de Calais area and whose pilots I had engaged that day.

We departed the building in a small open sedan. I was placed in the front seat to the right of the enlisted driver. The officer who greeted me and another officer were in the backseat, and an armed guard was seated in a jump seat. We drove some distance to a town and entered a building with a cathedral ceiling, tapestries on the walls, and nice furniture throughout. I was introduced by an officer-interpreter to two or three pilots whom he said had been engaged in the operation that day. One of these pilots, I noted, was redheaded, like me. I was offered a cigarette, which I accepted, and a glass of wine, which I declined. As I sat there, these pilots crowded around me trying to get me to say how and where I'd been in the fighting that day. All they knew was where I had crash-landed. They all appeared eager to get credit for an aerial victory. I was not in a very sociable mood, and since I really did not know where I was or where I had been, I could not have helped them even if I'd wanted to. I could just as well have been hit by flak. The interview did not last long, and I was soon packed into a car and driven to a large city that turned out to be Boulogne. I was delivered to the military police headquarters and locked up for the night in a small room with a bunk. This was a tough, no-nonsense outfit.

In 1968 the book *Horrido!* by Col. Raymond F. Toliver and Trevor J. Constable was published by Bantam. Page 291 describes a postwar interview with Gerhard Schöpfel, who tells the authors a story in order to illustrate the chivalry of the Luftwaffe. He recounts how one of his sergeant pilots who had red hair shot down an American named Clarke (sic) who was flying a Spitfire with the RAF. He says that this Clarke crash-landed on the coast of France and his pilot flew low over him and noted that Clarke also had red hair. Schöpfel arranged for them to meet that evening at their base, Fort Rouge, which was near Saint-Omer.

This account has the year wrong (1940 rather then 1942), and for reasons that I will explain, I don't believe that this redheaded German pilot was the one who actually shot me down. However, I believe I must be the Clark he was talking about. I have also recently exchanged correspondence with Gerhard Schöpfel. At the age of eighty-four and after years of being a POW of the Russians, he still remembers this incident. He stated in his letter that this young sergeant pilot was Hermann Meyer, who was killed in action in March of 1943 after gaining more than sixteen victories, each of which represented an airborne enemy aircraft destroyed.

To add further interest to this story, Donald Caldwell states in *JG 26* that Sergeant Meyer, leading a mission of eight aircraft, took off from Ducrat Airdrome at noon German time on this date to attack British aircraft circling low over the water northwest of Calais, fifteen miles north of Cape Gris-Nez where I crash-landed. Since my combat was at about the same time but way to the southwest of Abbéville in the vicinity of the Somme estuary, I don't see how we could have been involved in the same action. I believe he was either nearby, returning from that action north of Calais, and saw me when I slipped in and crash-landed unopposed, or he was called in to investigate after I landed. I am certain that I was unopposed from the time my engine started to "pack up" until I crash-landed. Then, since no one was able to claim me, he was given the credit, even after our evening chat. Sergeant Meyer's score that day, as reflected in the official Luftwaffe records for 26 July, credits him with two kills, one west of Boulogne and one south of Cape Gris-Nez (probably me). This gives one an interesting insight into the "flexibility" in the Luftwaffe victory credit system.

I am hopeful that someday I can learn more about JG26 operations on 26 July 1942 and tie down this interesting point. I do know that in the action north of Calais, the British lost three pilots, one a squadron leader, and the Germans lost four, including an ace with seventeen British aircraft to his credit. This latter pilot was not from JG26 but from a unit station farther north in Belgium and was flying an ME-109.

The records also show that the air/sea rescue units on both sides were active while this action was in progress. Caldwell says that Sergeant Meyer's pilots reported upon their return to base that they had attacked a high-speed British boat in the area and expressed some regret that it may have also been searching for a downed pilot. On the other hand, British reports indicate that two high-speed boats were attacked in the combat area and one was seen to be burning fiercely. So, all in all, it was a rather serious scrap, as the Brits would say.

CHAPTER 4

On to Dulag Luft, Ober Ursel

26 July to 30 July 1942

In the morning I was roughly aroused, given a razor and soap, led to a bathroom to clean up, and then driven to the train station in a car escorted by two Luftwaffe noncommissioned officers who were apparently going home on leave. I was given a brown paper bag containing some tough German bread and a slab of greasy pork fat. The train we boarded was called the Du Nord. I had never seen an American passenger car that could match this very modern, sleek, bright-red coach made all of steel. We were seated in a compartment by ourselves and promptly briefed by an army officer who was probably the train commander. He was an impressive-looking soldier in dress uniform, well decorated and wearing a steel helmet. I had an uneasy feeling that if the Germans could use an officer of his caliber just to be a train commander, this was going to be a long war.

From Boulogne we proceeded to Brussels, arriving in the afternoon. I was held for several hours in a station room where another young prisoner under guard was also being held. We were not allowed to communicate. He wore simple civilian clothes with a coat and tie, but he looked rather rough. I believe he was either a Slav or Pole, and he had some straw on his clothing as if he had been recently pulled out of a haystack.

Late in the evening we boarded a German second- or third-class coach filled with soldiers, women, and children, and we headed east into Germany. Every mile we went, I knew my chances of escape diminished. I looked long and hard at the big plate-glass window in our compartment, but I knew it would be a foolish act of desperation to dive through it. In any event, I was being carefully watched even when I went to the toilet at the end of the car.

There were no lights on in the train, it stopped often, and it was very crowded. At times during the night I had a baby on my lap. Sometime during the next day we passed slowly through a large city that I believe was Cologne, the site of the first British 1,000-bomber raid, which had taken place on 30 May. I guess everyone in our car knew that I was a POW, for they pulled down the shades on the windows to prevent me from seeing the damage that had been done to the city and its beautiful old cathedral.

We arrived in Frankfurt early the next morning, and I was escorted to the basement of another station room where about six RAF POWs were already gathered. They were sleeping on the only table and most of the chairs in the room, and my arrival aroused little curiosity. They were all as exhausted as I was. Later we were escorted to the large, marbled men's room where an old crone carefully handed each of us three sheets of toilet paper. After this long-over-due visit, we were put on a dinky little streetcar that took us up to the village of Ober Ursel, where Dulag Luft was located.

Dulag Luft was the Luftwaffe Interrogation Center for the Western theater of operations. All POWs captured by the Luftwaffe were brought there as soon after capture as possible. They were then interrogated for tactical information by a skilled intelligence officer or noncommissioned officer. This small, transient processing camp became familiar to almost all Allied airmen captured during the war, and only the Germans know how much useful information they obtained from us. It was probably considerable.

The camp was also useful in sorting out the new prisoners. The sick and wounded were sent up to the nearby POW hospital at the village of Hoemark, which was staffed by British doctors captured in France. Officers and enlisted men were sent on from there to separate camps, and all were given several shots, probably for typhus and tetanus. Clothing was issued to those in need. At that time, those services were administered by British Squadron Leader

Elliot, who was later joined by an American colonel, Charles Stark. The Germans were obviously pleased with the work of these two officers, because both were retained at Dulag Luft for the duration of the war. To my knowledge there were no escape attempts from the camp during their tenure, and they lived comfortably. This was a privilege that all of us who spent our years of captivity in a dirty, crowded main camp deeply resented, rightly or wrongly.

Our arrival at Dulag Luft was our introduction to our new life as prisoners of the Luftwaffe. We would come to know more about this place and its work as time passed. Every new prisoner, upon his later arrival at the permanent camps, was questioned by senior POWs to learn what the Germans were most interested in finding out at Dulag Luft, and this information was surreptitiously sent home to our intelligence people as an essential element of information.

The Germans maintained an efficient clipping service and had collected extensive personal and order-of-battle information by this means. It was not uncommon during this questioning for men, after stubbornly limiting their response to name, rank, and serial number, to be abruptly deflated when the Germans then told them details of their family, departure from the States, the name of their base, group, and squadron number, sometimes even showing them a copy of the mission order.

Upon arrival at Dulag Luft, all POWs were immediately thrown into solitary confinement. After a few days of this, loneliness, hunger, anxiety, and the craving for a cigarette took their toll. Some young men, still in shock from their traumas of survival and capture, were no match for a friendly but skilled German interrogator seeking to elicit information of value. The Germans had lots of experience in the extraction of information, and they worked at it, at least in our cases, without resorting to torture. Sometimes they deprived prisoners of food during interrogation and subjected them to alternatively over- and underheated cells for limited periods, but to my knowledge deliberate physical torture was not used on Allied POWs.

After the war one of the skilled noncommissioned interrogators became an American citizen and wrote a book about his work interrogating American fighter pilots in late 1943 and 1944. By then some very distinguished fighter aces and group commanders were being captured. His book makes it sound as though obtaining the information he wanted was not difficult. He kept some of these senior fighter pilots at Dulag Luft for days, taking them out on parole walks and visits to pubs for a beer together. He even arranged for one of them to fly an ME-109. The only purpose of all this in a total war, of course, was to gain information. I mention this to illustrate what a naive young American airman with limited resistance training was up against.

I was immediately placed in solitary confinement in a small cell with a bunk, chair, and a window with the shutters closed. I went through the usual preliminary interrogation exercise with a German NCO posing as a representative of the International Red Cross and wearing a Red Cross armband. He explained that filling out a form was necessary to inform my next of kin of my status. I stopped after name, rank, serial number, and the home address of my wife, which I gave as c/o Postmaster, San Antonio, Texas. This information plus my blood type and religious affiliation was on my dog tags, which they had confiscated. I was not pressed very hard for further information.

The next day a very quiet, gentlemanly officer came in and started a conversation that apparently convinced him I was not going to answer any important questions. Since the Germans had my aircraft, he knew I was flying with the British Tangmere Wing and that there were two possible reasons for my presence in Britain: either, as with so many other Americans, I was there to gain experience and then report back to some stateside training activity or I might be from one of the several U.S. fighter groups that the Germans knew had recently arrived in the United Kingdom. As the identifying letters on the sides of my aircraft had obviously been hastily changed from those of the 309th Squadron (WZB) of the 31st Group to those of the 412th Canadian Squadron (VZG), he may have already figured out who I was.

The only important question this officer asked me that I specifically remember, for he came in especially to ask it and then departed, was "Does the word *Bolero* mean anything to you?" Well, it did, as it was the code name of the secret program then in progress involving flying the U.S. fighter groups across the Atlantic to the United Kingdom via Greenland and Iceland using B-17s as mother ships. The B-17s did the navigating, with each one escorting six or eight fighters. I said, "No," and have no idea whether he believed me or not. In April and early May of 1942, the 31st Fighter Group was staging for the flight over, was stationed at Manchester, Vermont, and was equipped with P-39s. We had been scheduled to be the first unit to go over on Bolero, but our task force was disrupted by the Japanese attack on the Aleutian Islands. Our support bombers and cargo aircraft were pulled out in the middle of the night and sent to the West Coast. After a short delay we came over by ship, leaving our P-39s deserted on the airdrome.

P-38s of the 1st and 14th Fighter Groups were now coming over on Bolero. The interrogator's question simply illustrated how much the Germans knew. On 19 August, twenty-four days after I was shot down, the 31st Group entered combat as a full unit for the first time, in the Dieppe Raid. Their one-day involvement cost the group three pilots killed, one seriously injured and fished out of the Channel, and two prisoners of war. It is possible that only when the Germans questioned these two pilot POWs, who of course knew me well and believed me to be dead, were the Germans able to tie down my identity as the group executive of the 31st Group.

After about a week I was released from the interrogation unit and placed in the adjacent, small three-barrack compound. I was greeted by Squadron Leader Elliot, and he helped me get adjusted and provided me with essential toiletries. I then ran into a problem. The Germans confiscated my uniform. They claimed it was actually civilian clothing, but that was obviously not true, so this was pure harassment. Squadron Leader Elliot scrounged up a civilian striped Russian or Polish booty shirt and a pair of ill-fitting British army battle-dress trousers with suspenders for me. This was all the cloth-ing I had for the next several months.

Along with another new prisoner, a Canadian wing commander named McDonnell, I was taken on one escorted walk, accompanied by the same officer who had interrogated me. I sensed no effort to gain any information from us, except possibly to see how relations were between the Americans and Canadians. It wasn't long before I found myself "walking the circuit," as we called it. We walked end-lessly around the inside of the wire, much like the tigers and lions in the zoo. I formed up with a young Polish fighter pilot by the name of Pentz who had been recently shot down flying in one of several Polish squadrons in the Royal Air Force. My new Polish friend and I exchanged our "shoot down" stories and later ended up together in the East and then North Camps at Sagan. I have often wondered what became of him after the war, as returning to his utterly devas-tated country was a dismal prospect.

The story of the Polish Air Force is a tragic one. It was destroyed on the ground when the Germans struck Poland by sur-prise on 1 September 1939. The personnel were captured en masse, yet many somehow managed to escape within a year. With incred-ible hardship and adventures, they traveled in large groups to the eastern Mediterranean and took ships to France. They arrived too late to help the French Air Force, so they went on to England and were integrated into the RAF as Polish units.

Before long some of these men found themselves prisoners of war back in or near their homeland. All were fighting under assumed names to protect their families, who in some cases lived within a few miles of the prison camps. All of these soldiers were fearful of the threat to their families should their real identities be discovered. Needless to say, they were also fearful of the pressure the Germans could put on them to rat on their colleagues in the camps. More than 120 Polish officers were held in the North Camp at Stalag Luft III by the end of the war, and I'm not aware of any case in which one of them got into trouble for protecting his identity.

CHAPTER 5

On to Stalag Luft III, Sagan

10 August to 13 August 1942

Within a week the Germans had assembled enough new prisoners, all RAF officers except for me, to fill a third-class passenger coach, and we were shipped off to a permanent camp. This turned out to be Stalag Luft III, at the small town of Sagan, sixty miles north of Czechoslovakia in what was then Silesia. Silesia in those days had a common border with Poland and is now part of Poland. We were very crowded in this car and were heavily guarded. Our shoes were taken from us for the duration of the journey, and we sat on wooden seats for the two or three days and nights that it took to reach Sagan. The seats were in pairs, back to back, so we sat knee to knee. Above the seats were luggage racks.

I heard an interesting story told by a *kriegie* (the German term for a POW) who traveled to Sagan later in the war in such a coach. During his journey, the Germans allowed the *kriegies*, if they wished to and were small enough, to climb up and lie in the luggage racks so they could stretch out their legs. This lad's brother had been shot down some months before and was, as far as he knew, missing in action. While he was up in one of those racks he looked up to find his brother's name scribbled on the ceiling right above his head.

We arrived on a siding in the Sagan station during the night of about 13 August 1942, and in the morning we detrained and were marched through the pine woods, which we would come to know well. We followed a sandy path for about a quarter of a mile to the camp. I vividly remember this arrival and the stark scene that met my eyes: the barbed wire, the guard towers, the bare gray ground, and the weathered gray huts. I felt overwhelming sadness at the grim prospect of my uncertain future in this godforsaken place. Oberfeldwebel Hermann Glemnitz met our motley group and took us to the officers' compound under guard.

Aerial photograph of Stalag Luft III taken by U.S. photo reconnaissance aircraft in October 1944 after the tunnel escape of March of that year. The exit of the tunnel Harry is clearly visible as a light spot just across the road that bounds the north edge of Stalag Luft III and is opposite the North Camp. Courtesy of the Air Force Academy Library

CHAPTER 6

East Camp, Stalag Luft III

13 August 1942 to 27 March 1943

We would soon learn that Sergeant Glemnitz was the senior noncommissioned officer in charge of security. It was his job to prevent us from escaping or doing the numerous other things that were forbidden by German regulations. Prohibited were activities such as making fun of, insulting, disobeying, or attempting to bribe the German officers, administrative staff, or the guards with whom we would be in daily contact. We were prohibited from possessing radios, organizing rebellions, staging protest demonstrations, or damaging German property. The Germans were especially alert to any attempt on our part to fabricate equipment such as civilian clothing, false travel papers, maps, compasses, or tools to cut through the wire. Glemnitz was an older man with a strong, heavily lined face and piercing eyes. He seemed to be able to look right through you, especially if you were involved in some clandestine activity.

The officers' compound at Stalag Luft III contained almost all of the RAF officers who had been captured since the start of the war. There were about 600 of them. In an adjacent compound were all of their aircrews, totaling about 1,200 noncommissioned officers whom the Brits called "other ranks." In accordance with the Geneva Convention, these enlisted men selected a spokesman for dealing with the Germans since they had no officers in their own camp. Their leader was an outstanding senior noncommissioned officer by the name of Dixie Dean. Dean continued to lead these men throughout the war, encountering some extremely difficult times, especially toward the end. He was highly respected by his men and was decorated after the war by the British government.

Stalag Luft III had been in operation only since the previous April, when all RAF prisoners had been brought there from a number of camps scattered throughout Germany. About twelve Americans were there when it opened. All except one were in the RAF, having volunteered to serve with the British before the United States entered the war. Most of them were from the Eagle Squadrons. The one exception was a U.S. Navy lieutenant, John Dunn, who had been lost in April off the aircraft carrier *Wasp*, which was working with the British navy in antisubmarine work east of the Orkney Islands. He had become lost in bad weather, ditched his aircraft in the sea off the coast of Norway, and was captured along with his gunner.

As we approached the gate to the camp, a crowd gathered inside to welcome us and look for friends and squadron mates. It was a hot summer day, so I expected the men to be lightly clothed, but I was unprepared for the scruffy appearance of so many of the officer prisoners. Some were heavily bearded, barefooted, and clad only in homemade, ragged shorts. I was something of a curiosity,

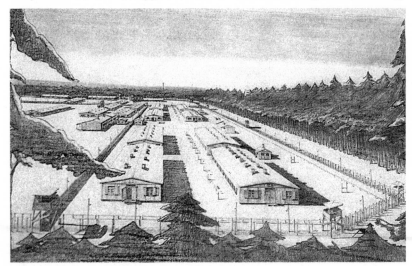

The East Camp at Stalag Luft III. Drawing by A. P. Clark

being a Yank and the youngest-looking lieutenant colonel they had ever seen. The growth of the U.S. Army Air Forces from about 2,000 officers in 1939 to its 1942 strength carried me along with all my contemporaries from captain to lieutenant colonel so fast that I don't ever remember wearing major's leaves. The first question I was asked, of course, was "How long is the war going to last?" When I said I expected it to last at least two years, my welcome cooled measurably.

The camp was cut out of a dense pine forest. The trees had been planted years before in regular rows. In all directions there was nothing to see except the trees. Everything in the camp was a dirty gray color: the unpainted, prefabricated wooden huts, the bare, sandy soil, the dense perimeter barbed wire, and the guard towers. Even the air that hung over the camp was always full of dust and smoke. There were eight huts, two latrines, and a kitchen building in the officers' compound and twelve huts and two kitchens in the enlisted men's compound. The two compounds were separated by a double barbed-wire fence and a solid board wall to inhibit communication between the officers and the enlisted men.

I was welcomed by the senior British officer (SBO), Group Capt. Marten Massy. He had flown in World War I and been injured. His injury had been aggravated when he was shot down and captured in 1941, and he walked with a cane. I was assigned to one of the two-man end rooms in one of the barracks. Its other occupant was Wing Commander Draper, who had been shot down the previous year. He had ditched his Spit in the Channel, and before he could get out of the cockpit he found himself plunging for the bottom. By the time he got clear of the aircraft, the water was so black he couldn't determine which way was up. Fortunately, his Mae West knew. His comrades called him "Blue to Black Draper."

Draper's roommate until about a week before I arrived had been Wing Comdr. Douglas Bader. Bader was famous for having been allowed by the Air Ministry to continue flying in combat despite the fact that he had lost most of both legs in a flying accident early in his career. He flew with well-fitted prostheses but lost them when he bailed out over France after what he claimed was a midair collision. Luftwaffe General Adolf Galland said it was a victory by one of his pilots, whom Bader had a chance to meet after the fight. The RAF dropped him a replacement set of aluminum legs by parachute, and he was able to walk quite well with a cane. He caused so much trouble in the camp by stirring up hostility and encouraging harassment of the Germans that they removed him to the punishment camp at Colditz Castle. I believe the SBO was relieved to see Bader go, as the ill will he generated between the prisoners and the Germans was becoming a serious problem, interfering with necessary daily routines such as getting the food and mail in and the garbage out of the camp.

In the corner of our small room was an iron stove on a tile base. Around it in five wooden casks was a brew of wine made from the rations of raisins and sugar collected from all of the one hundred men in the barrack block. The brewing was attended to by a Czech RAF pilot who had been a wine merchant in Prague before the war. The casks were covered with wet cloths and masses of flies. When our brewer said the wine was ready, the block threw a party. It happened only four days after my arrival.

Several invited guests who lived elsewhere in camp, including Wing Commander Day, joined us that night. Day was Harry Melville Arbuthnot Day, widely known as "Wings" Day. He was one of the oldest prisoners in the camp and one of the first captured in the war. All of the guests had themselves locked into our block for the night, and the wine was gone by midnight. As a new *kriegie*, I found that this was a rough way to be introduced to the stresses, anxieties, and inhibitions that years in this wretched environment generated. We all got drunk and it turned into a wild night. By morning most of us were very sick. A couple of fights ensued, and one poor soul went out the window to take his chances with the night sentries and their dogs as the lesser of the evils. I helped "Doctor" Libby sew up a scalp cut on one unfortunate fellow who received a blow from a gymnasium Indian club. My job was to hold the inebriated patient down.

Wings Day spent the final few hours before daylight making a speech to Draper and me. He was standing on a stool in our small, crowded room speaking of great heroics while we were trying to sleep. He was the only man among us that I can remember who wasn't throwing up out the windows as soon as we were unlocked. Wings was one of the few men in camp who had seen service in World War I. In fact, he had been decorated for heroism as a Marine lieutenant for rescuing men trapped below deck on a sinking British battleship. He had then served actively in the RAF and was commanding a Blenheim reconnaissance squadron in France when the war started on 3 September 1939. On 13 October he led his squadron's first mission into Germany and was shot down. He was highly respected, almost revered, by the British prisoners for his leadership, fatherly advice, and his numerous escape attempts. The full story of his five and a half years as a prisoner in Germany has been published in the book *Wings Day* by Sydney Smith.

There was a quiet little French Catholic priest in our camp by the name of Father Goodreau who had trained to spend his life as a missionary in Basutoland, now part of South Africa. He was en route in 1939 on the steamship *Zam Zam* when the ship was one of the first lost to a German submarine off Africa, and he was taken to Germany on the sub as an intern. He volunteered to serve for the duration in a British POW camp and ended up at Stalag Luft III. At war's end (almost six years later) when I said good-bye to him, he said he would go on to Basutoland as planned. We exchanged Christmas cards for some years. Basutoland was a primitive country of grass-shack villages which he served riding from village to village on a donkey. Father Goodreau retired back to Canada in about 1980.

Shortly after my arrival in camp, I was taken for a walk around the perimeter by Maj. Johnny Dodge, a very kind gentleman who was the only British army officer among us. He was known as "The

Dodger," because of his many escape attempts. Johnny had a colorful background. He was American-born and was a nephew (by marriage) of Winston Churchill. He had distinguished himself in action in the First World War, was wounded twice, and had received the Distinguished Service Cross for his bravery at Gallipoli. In 1940 he was serving as a major with the gallant 51st Highland Regiment in France. When France fell, the whole regiment was captured in spite of a brave effort by Johnny to get a ship to take them off. Somehow he ended up in Luftwaffe hands and remained so until he fell into the hands of the Gestapo after escaping in the tunnel break of March 1944. The Germans sent him into Switzerland before the end of the war with a message from Himmler to his uncle in a useless effort to get Britain to make peace and "help the Germans to save Europe from the barbarians from the East." Johnny Dodge gave me one of my most treasured possessions—a pair of flannel pajamas.

I soon learned that our basic treatment and living conditions were set forth in considerable detail in the articles of the Geneva Convention of 1929, to which the United States, Britain, and Germany, among other nations, were signatories. There were ninety-seven provisions and, if complied with, they provided reasonably for the war prisoners' welfare. I had never heard of these provisions but would become quite familiar with them, as they were the subject of endless complaints and arguments between the *kriegies* and the German authorities.

There were three international agencies dedicated to assisting U.S. POWs. A protecting power, the Swiss government in our case, had been selected by both Germany and the United States to deal with issues involving violations of the Geneva Convention or other serious issues between the prisoners and the detaining power. The International Red Cross assumed responsibility for providing food, clothing, and medical supplies to meet the basic needs of prisoners in countries where their presence was permitted. An exception was Russia, where Stalin regarded the Red

Cross as an espionage organization and declined its offer to assist the 3 million Russian prisoners in Germany. The third organization involved was the International YMCA, which provided Allied prisoners in Germany with books for libraries, sports equipment, musical instruments, and equipment for religious services. Representatives of all three of these organizations visited our camps regularly, listened to our complaints, took note of our needs, undertook to alleviate our problems through negotiations with the German authorities, and sent us prodigious amounts of food, equipment, and supplies throughout the war.

I personally had few contacts with these representatives except for Henry Soderberg, who was the YMCA representative for the Allied camps in the northwestern part of Germany. He was a young Swedish lawyer, was dedicated to his work, and he became well known and respected in every camp that he served. His passport was signed by the King of Sweden, giving him remarkable freedom to travel in Germany. I became close friends with Henry after the war, and he was always invited to our reunions, which he seldom missed. In 1985 I visited him and his wife in Sweden and arranged for the bulk of his papers covering his wartime work to be acquired by the Air Force Academy Library. They include his official reports, several photo albums, his own diaries of visits to the camps, and records of his difficult work with the German authorities. It is a priceless collection of an important aspect of the POW story.

Henry Soderberg, the young Swede who represented the International YMCA, which serviced our camp throughout the war. Courtesy of the Air Force Academy Library

In about September, I was approached by John Casson, one of the few naval officers in the camp. He had been shot down in an attack on German warships early in the war flying a Swordfish, an antiquated biplane torpedo bomber with which the British navy started the war. John's father and mother were both well known on the legitimate stage in London, and he reflected this talent in our camp plays. He sought me out to introduce me to the camp's most secret activity—the code work that we used via the mail to keep in touch with British intelligence. He taught me the coding procedure, assigned me my own personal code key word, and before long I received a message from a member of the RAF Women's Air Force (WAF) whom I was to pretend to have known during my brief stay in England. I wrote to her reporting the number of American POWs in camp and eventually received an answer from 8th Air Force intelligence. I decoded it with great expectation of a substantive message, possibly with instruction to collect and report some essential information. I was disgusted to find a message that read something like "B-17s bombing from altitude with great accuracy and shooting down many enemy fighters." This was sheer propaganda and was not true at that time, as we prisoners certainly knew. It was an insult to our intelligence.

I used this secret channel very sparingly, as it was basically a British system, and, as a senior officer, I had to maintain a high profile. Code work was espionage, and punishment would be quite severe if I were caught. The method of inserting a coded message in our letters was quite complicated. It involved a matrix of letters within which each code worker's own personal five-letter code word was embedded. We were always prepared to eat the secret reference material in the event that we were surprised by the Germans. Long messages were difficult to send in the three small German-issued one-page letters and four postcards allowed each month. Later, we organized well-educated, low-profile men into a room by themselves to do this work under the direct supervision of the senior American officer (SAO). They got so good at it that they were able to encode and decode messages without using any reference material, and thus were quite secure.

It was already October, and I had received no mail. Since I had learned from later arrivals that I had been reported killed, I was terribly anxious to get verification that my wife, Carolyn, and my three children knew that I was alive. This was an agony of uncertainty. While mail to the camp arrived at unpredictable times and usually by the carload from Switzerland or Sweden, some men were always getting mail, especially some of the old British *kriegies*. There was no limit on how much a *kriegie* could receive, but outgoing mail was strictly limited. I had been sending my limit every month since my arrival at Dulag Luft in early August.

☆   ☆   ☆

The summer of 1942 was very hot and dry in Germany, and we were overwhelmed by the flies. They were breeding in the filthy, primitive latrines, and slugs were crawling around the camp spreading dysentery and skin diseases. Since there were no window or door screens in the camp, we had to have a "fly purge" prior to eating our principal meal each day. We opened wide the one window of our room, and then lined up shoulder to shoulder along the opposite wall with our bath towels, moving slowly toward the window while waving them. The flies would flee out the window in a dark cloud, after which we slammed it shut and ate quickly.

Neither the Germans nor the Brits seemed to care about this unsanitary situation, and the RAF had obviously not trained its personnel to deal with such matters. Worrying about "the loos," as the latrines were called, was not something for officers to be concerned with. Fortunately, I had spent two summers at Fort Logan, Colorado, during the years when the Civilian Conservation Corps (CCC) was providing employment to many thousands of men who were jobless as a result of the Great Depression. My father was the surgeon at the post and, as such, was responsible for the health and well-being of these men in the camps throughout Colorado. I often accompanied Dad when he inspected the camps, and I learned what a clean and fly-proof latrine should look like and how it should be constructed.

I therefore volunteered to fix our latrines and received the approval of a somewhat perplexed SBO. I called for volunteers, and the Australians, New Zealanders, South Africans, and Canadians quickly stepped forward, but no Englishmen. With tools provided by the Germans after my assurances that they would not be used for escape purposes, we sealed the pits to flies, put a stack over them to remove the odors, and put screens on the doors and windows. The flies disappeared, and the illnesses cleared up. Some clown dubbed it "Clark's Crap in Comfort Campaign." The Germans incorporated these improvements in the latrines of all four of the future compounds built at Stalag Luft III, and the commandant mentioned my work in his memoirs.

☆　☆　☆

On a number of occasions during this summer, formations of German workers were marched past our camp to some work site back in the woods to the south. These were all well-disciplined young men of the *Arbeit Dienst* (the Works Corps). They were not in the army, but were obviously well trained. They wore white work uniforms and marched proudly and with élan. They carried shovels over their shoulders in perfect alignment and sang their marching songs with great gusto. The shovels appeared to be shined. As I watched these men, I couldn't help wondering how Germany could still use this quality of young men just to dig holes, and I feared we were faced with a long war.

As time passed, we learned more about the way the Russian POWs in the army camp to the west of ours—in fact all Russian prisoners in Germany—were being mistreated. After the war large mass graves were found in the woods south of that camp, and I suspect that the *Arbeit Dienst* workers were digging those grave pits. During the previous year huge battles had raged on the eastern front and the Germans were capturing masses of Russian prisoners. They were shipped back to Germany locked in boxcars with little or no attention. Sometimes those who survived the trip were dumped in a wooded area surrounded by barbed wire and the ubiquitous watchtowers. They dug holes in the ground, resorted to cannibalism, and in a few months they had all perished. It is hard to believe, but 2 million Russian prisoners died of neglect in German captivity during the war. The Germans regarded the Russians and the Poles as *untermenchen* (inferior human beings) and justified their deliberate genocidal policies on this basis.

There was seldom any activity outside our wire that drew our interest—nothing but pine trees in every direction. Early in the morning we sometimes heard the large, dark cuckoo birds calling, and one day a young one came into the camp and was fed and handled for a while. Little events like this were long remembered. Later in the war when the ration of coal for the civilian population of Sagan was probably very meager, the authorities allowed women to gather wood in the forest near our camp. They would load their carts with every little twig, always leaving the forest quite clear of any underbrush. Alas, these women were all middle-aged *Hausfrau* and not much to look at.

One day, however, a lovely young woman showed up near the wire and walked slowly around the camp. We immediately noticed that the attention of one of our Czech officers was riveted on her. He slowly followed her around the camp from inside the wire without any conversation between them. She must have been his wife or fiancée. After the war, Glemnitz told me that he had allowed her to do this and had notified the Czech officer that she was there. I never learned the whole story, but it was a very unusual and poignant encounter. Unfortunately, this officer was lost in the tunnel escape in March of 1944.

☆ ☆ ☆

By the end of August, six officers from the U.S. armed forces were in the East compound. Lt. John Dunn had been the first to arrive. He was a Naval Academy graduate. He accepted his bad luck with dignity and humor. I was the next to arrive in camp, but actually was the third to have been taken prisoner. Second Lt. Marshall Draper was the second to be captured and the third to arrive, having come from the hospital. He almost died in the surf after his aircraft was shot down while exiting Holland on the disastrous Fourth of July Kagelman Raid. The fourth U.S. airman to be taken prisoner was an NCO tail gunner named Morris whose B-24 was part of the Halverson Project, which was bombing shipping in the Mediterranean. He fell into the sea in the tail section of the aircraft, which had separated from the rest of the falling bomber. As our army was not yet even in the theater, much less in action, the first American prisoners were all airmen until after the invasion of North Africa in November.

Next to join us in camp were my two group mates, Lt. Ed Tovrea and Lt. Buck Inghram, who were shot down during the Dieppe Raid on 19 August. Both Ed and Buck spent some time in their dinghies before being picked up by the Germans. At Dulag Luft during interrogation, they may have inadvertently helped the Germans confirm my association with the 31st Group. They had been led to believe that I was dead, so they were unable to avoid displaying surprise when told that I was a prisoner. Then came Lt. Tex Newton. He was the pilot of one of the early B-24s shot down in the Mediterranean in late August, and he arrived from the hospital in the fall. He had ditched his aircraft in the sea and lost half his crew in the process. Tex was a talented country-music fiddler, and all through the war he made important contributions to our morale. After the war he became an ordained Baptist minister.

I came to realize that our group was unique. We were survivors of a series of screening and selection processes that were most unusual. First we had volunteered to go to war as aviators. We had been found qualified after a demanding selection process, had graduated from a dangerous flight training program with a high attrition rate, had gone off to war, entered combat, and then survived a traumatic disaster in the air. There was no other way to join this group. We were different. Our experiences had left a mark on us that would remain for the rest of our lives. By nature more group oriented, we assisted each other in an unusually generous and understanding way. We were cheerful and often were involved in hilarious stunts and practical jokes. And we sometimes took incredible risks to escape or to support other clandestine activities.

These early arrivals provided examples of the extraordinary survival experiences of typical American airmen prisoners. No two were exactly alike. It never occurred to me that these men would be followed into the German prison camps by more than 40,000 others before the war was over. Considering the variety of their harrowing experiences, by the war's end it could truthfully be said that whatever a man could experience and survive had happened at least once during the war. There were many instances of men being blown out of exploding aircraft at high altitude. Unconscious initially, they often regained their senses barely in time to open their parachutes and reach the ground safely. There were so many of these incidents that such a survivor found it difficult to hold an audience's attention long enough to complete his "there I was" story. There were even a few cases of men falling from great heights without parachutes and surviving.

With the enthusiastic support of eight of the early birds, I decided to establish the first all-American room. I wasn't too happy where I had been billeted as the only Yank in a barracks full of Brits, and since I was quite senior, close and warm relationships were hard to establish. So in September I joined Dunn, Draper, Tovrea, Inghram, and Newton along with three Americans who had been flying with the RAF—Pilot Officers Bill Geiger, Arvin Granger McDaniels (at age eighteen, one of our few teenagers), and Bernard Meyers—and opened "Little America" in the same block with the Polish officers. I could have moved into the adjacent two-man room, but since the camp policy reserved these rooms for senior officers and we had no others above the grade of first lieutenant, I declined and moved in with the lieutenants. Wing Comdr. Stanford Tuck and Squadron Leader Roger Bushell, who later was the mastermind of the escape committee, promptly moved into this end room and joined our mess.

Tucky, as he was called, was a slender, dark-haired, handsome man, rather dapper and, I would guess, an accomplished ladies' man. He was one of the heroes of the Battle of Britain and not a very profound or serious-minded person. Roger Bushell, on the other hand, was a brilliant and very sophisticated man. He was a barrister by profession and a member of the RAF reserves. He had traveled extensively in Europe, skied in Switzerland, and he spoke fluent German. He never missed an opportunity to practice, and many times that fall and winter he stood at our open window after lockup and chatted with Charlie the ferret (a ferret was a German guard specially trained to root out escape activity). Charlie was an incorruptible and very savvy German enlisted man who had found tunnels at Barth before coming to Sagan. He continued to be one of the sharpest of the ferrets and a constant thorn in our side.

From the Red Cross parcels we usually managed a breakfast of tea or coffee, one slice of the very unattractive German bread toasted and spread with German margarine, and German ersatz honey or marmalade. For the noon meal we usually collected a German hot soup at the cookhouse. Sometimes it was wholesome, but often it was made from inferior products such as rotting potatoes, weevil-infested grain, and on a few occasions, virtually the entire carcass of an old cow, including the head. The soup was cooked in a huge coal-burning pressure cooker into which the ingredients were shoveled by the wheelbarrow load. While it was often repulsive, we consumed it, since it had at least been well cooked. For supper we usually made up a dish from our parcels, which were pooled for the room. This would often be a canned meat product with potatoes that we cooked with the meat. When the American parcels started arriving, the meat was either Spam or corned beef. Frequently we would make a pie with raisins, apple-sauce, or chocolate mixed with whipped powdered milk. When parcels came regularly, we were adequately nourished, combining what we received from the Germans and the Red Cross. Without the Red Cross food parcels we would have slowly starved to death.

Wing Comdr. Stanford Tuck of Battle of Britain fame with Roger Bushell, the brilliant officer in charge of escape activities in the North Camp, on right. Courtesy of the Air Force Academy Library

From time to time we were unable to eat items from the German ration. Among these were rutabagas and kohlrabies, essentially large turnips or cabbages that were cattle food. They were as hard as wood, and no amount of cooking made them edible. We didn't want the Germans to know that we weren't eating them, since we feared they might reduce our rations, so we took these vegetables out and buried them. Some were thrown into the latrine pits, but that practice came back to bite us when the unfortunate Polish "honey wagon" driver who emptied these pits had to dig the huge things out. The Germans gave us a bad time when that happened. Another delicacy we couldn't eat was a cheese that smelled just like rotten fish. The Poles seemed to be able to cook with it, but we buried it. We had to get it out of the block very quickly or it would drive us out. The Germans also issued us blood cheese, which was rather repulsive looking but quite nourishing. Though most of us would eat it, there were some who wouldn't touch it even in the most difficult times. They suspected that it might be made from the sweepings off the slaughterhouse floor.

As the senior American officer, I represented my small but rapidly growing group of Yanks on matters affecting our welfare. I accompanied the SBO and members of his staff to regular meetings with the German commandant out front in the *Vorlager* (outer camp) where all of the German offices, barracks, and other assorted buildings were located. At that time, the German garrison numbered about eight officers, fifteen noncommissioned officers, and possibly 200 men. Most of them were not qualified for front-line duty as the result of age, wounds, or other factors. They would have been called category 4-F at home.

The first time I participated in the routine *Vorlager* meetings I was amazed at the antics of Wings Day. While we were alone in the room for a few minutes, he immediately unscrewed several light-bulbs from the table lamps and put them in his pockets. At one meeting the Germans complained that the British officers were putting razor blades in potatoes in the garbage to kill German pigs. The British position was that while they did not acknowledge the charge, the garbage was their property. After this pronouncement Major Zimoliet, the deputy commandant, recounted the story about the war between two towns in ancient Greece that was caused because a man in one town sold a donkey to a man from the other town but refused to agree that the donkey's shadow was part of the deal.

The camp commandant, Col. Friedrich Wilhelm Von Lindeiner-Wildau, was an impressive old gentleman: tall, clean-cut, and an officer of the old school. He was sixty-one years old and had an impressive record of service from World War I. While he was known to be anti-Nazi, like many other Germans he knew that active resistance was a death warrant. He was married to a Dutch woman, and consequently his future in the German military service was clouded. Eventually, having been refused retirement, he was given command of Stalag Luft III, a job that would accelerate his aging process. Few of us knew about or appreciated his efforts to keep the camp from being taken over and managed by

Heinrich Himmler and his wretched Gestapo. Lindeiner knew that our escape record could be his undoing, and he tried to convince our senior people a number of times to recognize the peril to all of us. He operated on the assumption that if he treated us well enough, our escape efforts would diminish. He was tragically wrong.

The British huts were disheveled and untidy, in striking contrast to the conditions in the American hut, which was generally fairly neat. Part of this was deliberate on the part of the old British prisoners, some of whom had been "in the bag" since early in the war. They were simply making it as difficult as possible for the Germans

Col. Friedrich Wilhelm von Lindeiner was the commandant of Stalag Luft III from its opening until he was removed from command after the mass escape of March 1944. German photograph, courtesy of the Air Force Academy Library.

during their endless surprise searches. One day Colonel Lindeiner answered a written request from the SBO for more cleaning materials—brushes, brooms, and so forth—by pointing out that where there was a will to be clean, it was possible with a minimum of materials. He then went on to cite the American hut as an example of what he meant. His comment was deeply resented by the Brits, and we all suspected him of simple troublemaking. On another occasion the men in one hut were accused of insulting one of the ferrets who was trying to perform an impromptu search of their busy kitchen. The ferret went out in a huff and shortly thereafter a wagon pulled by two horses came galloping up. Two Germans went into the hut, ripped out the smoking stove with food still in the oven, put it in the wagon, and galloped out of the camp followed by hoots, cheers, and catcalls from the POWs.

☆ ☆ ☆

In about September, Wally Floody, a Canadian fighter pilot who had been shot down in October of 1941, asked me if I would like to do some tunneling. He had experience working in the Canadian gold mines and was soon digging tunnels, first at Stalag Luft I, at Barth on the Baltic coast, and then at Stalag Luft III at Sagan. Wally was a tall, thin cadaverous-looking man. Later, after almost a year underground designing, supervising, and digging the tunnels in North Camp for the large escape of 24 March 1944, Wally looked terrible: pale and gaunt, with deep-sunken eyes.

Wally and his crew had been working on a shallow tunnel from hut 67 northeast to the corner of the cookhouse. This tunnel was not shored due to its small cross section of just less than two square feet. It had a branch that was supposed to connect hut 67 with hut 66, which was opposite 67 on the other side of the center north-south road through the camp. This branch had been abandoned because of the threat of a cave-in; the Germans had begun driving the heavy fire truck around the camp trying to cause the collapse of our tunnels. The abandoned branch was subsequently used to store sand from the face of the main tunnel (the point at which active digging was taking place). Avoiding the disposal of sand above-ground was most desirable, as the sand we excavated was pale yellow in color and stood out in contrast to the dirty gray loam and surface debris common to this pine forest area.

When I joined the tunnelers, the tunnel had passed the corner of the cookhouse and turned east for the last short stretch to the wire. Another branch had been dug under the cookhouse's brick floor leading to a large, empty space where all remaining sand could be deposited. We worked from lockup at night until unlock in the morning. The entrance, which we called the trap, was located under the center of one of the rooms over a blocked area where the ferrets couldn't crawl when checking for traps under the hut. The Germans had left about two feet of headroom under most huts so they could crawl around and probe for traps that started through the floor above.

We worked in long underwear, and when I returned to my room by a devious route in the early mornings, I stopped at the wash house en route and took a cold shower. I then dropped the sand-stained "long johns" into a bucket of water lest the Germans call a surprise search of our hut and discover them.

Working underground in these tunnels was not for the claustrophobic. Except at the face or when we had fat lamps, we often worked without light, and communication was very difficult. We had several cave-ins, but no casualties, only a few instances when we had to pull someone out by his heels. The air was foul, and often, toward the end of the night, the air got so bad that the fat lamps would go out and we would emerge in the morning with severe headaches. This is why in the old days miners used to carry a canary down with them: if the air was bad and the canary died, it was time to get out.

I was working under the cookhouse floor one night, passing sand from the face to other tunnelers farther up the branch, when the *Hund Fuhrer* (guard with a dog) noisily brought his Alsatian into the cookhouse to rest and warm up. He sat down very close to where I was working, and his dog wandered about the floor over my head. I was only the thickness of a brick beneath him, and I could hear the sniffing and the clicking of his dog's claws on the floor. I remained absolutely still, but I could sense the dog's interest in the spot right above me. He undoubtedly smelled me or the fresh sand that I was handling. Eventually the guard and his dog departed, but the next day the Germans knocked a hole in the floor at that spot and discovered our tunnel. That tunnel was one of about one hundred that the Germans discovered at Stalag Luft III before we were hurriedly evacuated ahead of the advancing Russian forces on 27 January 1945.

I had gotten to know Roger Bushell quite well since he and Stanford Tuck had joined our mess. After his working over by the Gestapo, Roger kept a low profile and left the escape activity to Commdr. Jimmy Buckley, Royal Navy. In October, however, the

Germans selected Buckley and about one hundred British *kriegies* to be sent to a camp at Shubin in Poland, designated Oflag 64 and under army jurisdiction. Wings Day volunteered to go along as he was restless, and Group Captain H. M. Massey had arrived and become the SBO at Stalag Luft III.

The Germans believed that they were sending away the most active escapees in our group, and they were close to the mark. Those *kriegies* began escape activity while they were en route to Poland, and when they arrived at Shubin they had almost completed cutting a hole through the floor of the goods car in which they were locked for the journey. They were quite successful in their escape work at Shubin. About thirty men got away in a tunnel break, and among them were Wings Day himself and Commander Buckley. Most were promptly recaptured and eventually returned to Sagan. Buckley's plan was to go to Sweden by way of Denmark. Some months later we got the sad news that his body had washed up on the coast of Denmark.

There is a wonderful story told by Wings Day in Sydney Smith's book, *Wings Day*. He says that upon arrival at Shubin, Sergeant Glemnitz, who had headed the guard detail on the trip, reported to the German army commandant and tried to warn him that his charges, who were waiting under guard out in front of the camp gates, were very determined escapees. Glemnitz told the commandant that he would do well to take certain precautions that he, Glemnitz, would be pleased to pass on to him. The commandant apparently told Glemnitz he needed no help from the Luftwaffe, as the army knew very well how to handle prisoners. Glemnitz came back out livid with rage and told his group of prisoners good-bye, describing to them the rude way he had been treated and urging them to "escape, escape, escape!"

By early fall of 1942 I had learned that, ruling out a balloon, there were basically only three ways to escape from Stalag Luft III: through a tunnel, through or over the wire, or through the gate. We had developed active plans to use all three of these methods. I had also come to understand that not everyone in the camp was fired up over the idea of escape, but everyone *was* prepared to assist others through our highly organized efforts. Everyone clearly understood the need for security, which meant no curiosity or loose talk about activities related to escape.

About 60 percent of the *kriegies* were deeply involved in some capacity in the escape effort: digging, making false papers, maps, compasses, civilian clothing, collecting necessary information, or protecting these activities with an elaborate security system. When not planning escape, there were other activities to keep us occupied. About 40 percent of those in the camp studied, read books, and participated in organized literary and educational activities or sports. Many also worked hard in vital functions necessary to keep the camp running smoothly. In this respect, the camp operated like a military unit with administrative, supply, maintenance, cookhouse, and medical staffs working daily with their German counterparts.

The escape efforts achieved several spectacular near-successes during the summer of 1942, before my arrival. For example, there were a couple of near "walk outs." Bob VanDerStok, a Dutch officer serving in the RAF as a fighter pilot, had fought for Holland and after its fall had escaped to Britain and volunteered to fly for the RAF. He spoke fluent German and almost cleared the camp disguised as a German guard. Equipped with a false gate pass, he talked his way through two of the three gates and was unfortunate enough to run into the German sergeant he was impersonating. I believe Wings Day, with two companions, also attempted a walk out before I arrived, but Wings was recognized at the gate and ended up in the cooler for two weeks. He was tall, gangling, and easy to spot.

I should mention that among the RAF officers who were assembled at Stalag Luft III when it opened was a group sent from a British army officers' camp at Warburg. Most had been captured at Dunkirk and they ran a well-organized camp with an active escape committee. The RAF officers participated and brought with them some sophisticated skills and ideas to make our escape and intelligence activities more effective. Several had experience in forging passes, passports, and travel papers. Others could transform a uniform into passable civilian wear and knew how to handle dyes and bleaches. In light of its growing sophistication, the X (escape) committee, which included several Americans though it was basically a British show, was becoming a formidable threat to the Germans who were charged with keeping us in.

There were about six Americans in camp who had been shot down flying with the Brits in one of the three Eagle Squadrons. They had volunteered for this service prior to the U.S. entry into the war. (In September of 1942 those American airmen still active in the RAF were transferred en masse to the United States Air Force and became the 4th Fighter Group, which went on to distinguish itself in combat.) In the summer of 1942, one of the Eagle Squadron pilots named Nichols and a British companion, Ken Toft, walked calmly into the perimeter wire in broad daylight, cut their way through with wire cutters, and walked away. The key to their success was a couple of effective diversions of the guards in the goon boxes (guard towers) on each side of their point of approach to the wire. These diversions involved, on one side, a spectacular fight and shouting match near the guard rail (the dead line about ten feet from the wire fence beyond which the guards would fire at a trespassing *kriegie*) and, on the other side, a dramatic fainting spell that drew a crowd. The boredom of duty in the goon boxes made these guards quite vulnerable to distractions. Nichols and Toft were not gone long, but they earned the admiration of even the Germans for their cool and well-planned effort. They had discovered that there was a blind spot once they reached the wire where no guard could see them. After that the Germans built extensions on the tower platforms to give their goons a better view of the inner circumference of the wire.

Three other *kriegies*, with the help of a crowd of sunbathers, managed to dig themselves into a shallow tunnel starting in a drainage ditch near the east perimeter wire. They were then sealed in, and they dug ahead, passing the dirt back and filling behind them until they got beyond the wire. It took them about fourteen hours, but they made it and were gone for ten days. We called this a "mole job," and the technique was repeated again from this same camp in 1943 in the famous Wooden Horse escape. Three men started their tunnel under a gymnasium vaulting horse that was brought out to the same spot near the "circuit" (the walking path around the camp just to the camp side of the dead line rail) each day for exercise. The horse was supported by a large wooden skirt. There was enough space inside this skirt to conceal the tunnelers, and each day when the horse was brought back in, it contained the tunnelers plus freshly excavated dirt. Eventually they had enough space in the tunnel to seal themselves in and mole the rest of the way. After escaping the camp, the three made their way to Sweden.

☆　☆　☆

During the winter, the American group continued to grow. By March 1943 we had about 160 officers. Many of the new arrivals had been captured in Africa. They arrived after a dangerous flight in German transports from Africa to Italy then a long, dangerous train trip up across Italy and through the Brenner Pass locked in crowded boxcars and exposed to bombing and malnutrition. Many had been wounded or infected with hepatitis by the time they arrived. While the yellow-fever shots they had received from our own medics often produced a jaundice of some sort, it was thought that the cause of most of the hepatitis was water from Italian wells poisoned by the retreating Germans. We also had several cases of strep throat. None of these sick men received any treatment, and eventually they recovered on their own.

Considering the circumstances we were in, our general health was extraordinarily good. We were all physically fit young men who had qualified for flying, and we were, in effect, in quarantine. I have often thought that we offered a marvelous test group for a

Majors W. C. Beckham and David M. Jones (right). Beckham was an ace fighter pilot with the Silver Star Medal and Davy was a flight commander on the Doolittle Raid against Japan in April of 1942 with the Distinguished Flying Medal. Courtesy of the Air Force Academy Library

health study. No one was obese, there was no booze, no women, no drugs, and damned little sugar.

In November 1942, I became aware of an irregularity in my pulse, and I approached the British doctor. He arranged for me to be taken in an ambulance— under guard, of course—into Sagan to a doctor's office where a very unpleasant lady recorded my heart on an electrocardiogram. The problem turned out to be a harmless form of extra systole, and I quit worrying about it, but on Christmas Day I stopped smoking and regard that decision as one of the best I made during the entire war.

☆   ☆   ☆

As Little America grew in numbers, I put the men to work, trying as best I could to match the work assignment with the talents and experience of each man. We started interviewing new arrivals, first to establish their bona fides and then to develop a card file of their skills and talents which might be useful to the community in some way. With the passage of time and with a growing reservoir of talents, education, and experience, we seldom had a need that wasn't immediately filled by a volunteer who met the requirements.

One man whom I put to work right away was Maj. David Jones. I have vivid memories of when he arrived, having been shot down in Africa on 12 December 1942. He'd been one of General Doolittle's flight commanders on the April raid against mainland Japan, and he was the next field grade officer in camp. He began building secret hiding places for the camp's growing inventory of civilian-type clothing and such items. We had noted that the partitions separating the rooms in the blocks were thin, prefabricated double-wood panels with a paper-felt liner. We found that we could

Capt. John Bennett. Courtesy of the Air Force Academy Library

carefully separate these panels by about a foot, thus creating a large storage space that was very difficult for the ferrets to detect. It simply made the room a foot smaller. We had to be extremely careful doing this. Good security during the construction was paramount because of the constant risk of an unexpected visit from a ferret who may have heard the hammering. Also, new nails replaced in the wall with shiny heads or the general appearance of new work could give the show away, and that

Tex Newton. Portrait by Pat Holmstrom. Courtesy of Tex Newton

would result in the loss of our inventory of items acquired through lots of hard, dangerous, and difficult work.

Jones was a real leader and was very well liked by all of us. He participated in the square dance that we put on for the Brits and became our first block commander. The square dance was a

The American krieges *put on an American square dance for the Brits. Courtesy of the Air Force Academy Library*

huge success. Half the group dressed up as women and some were quite attractive. Tex Newton made an excellent hillbilly fiddler and Capt. John Bennett called the dances in a most professional manner.

John Bennett was a big, strong, handsome man. Although suffering from a wounded leg and a badly sprained ankle, he evaded capture for a week after parachuting into France on 21 October 1942. He was a skilled craftsman and was soon involved making excellent little compasses. He volunteered for any job needing to be done. He became infected with hepatitis while helping me with a latrine project and was quite ill for a while. He would be among the experienced cadre we sent over to help West Camp get squared away when it opened in 1944.

☆ ☆ ☆

I had still received no mail, but had continued writing home as frequently as my allowance of three letters and four postcards per month would allow. I had no way of knowing whether Carolyn knew that I was alive. This was one of the most agonizing aspects of my time as a prisoner. Then, on Christmas Day 1942, five months after my capture, I was called out by Haupman Von Massau, the local intelligence staff officer. He wanted to walk the circuit with me, and he questioned me about Charles Lindbergh. Von Massau wanted to know how strong a following Lindbergh had in the United States. I told him that Lindbergh had been a man of great stature in our country, but his opposition to the war fell on deaf ears after the Pearl Harbor attack and the commencement of the war with Germany. Von Massau then handed me three letters from Carolyn. I think he'd been holding them for some time. Now, at last, I could relax a little with the knowledge that my family knew I was alive. It was a tremendous relief.

We were not eating well, as the only parcels were from the British Red Cross and they didn't cater to American tastes. The parcels contained the thoroughly unpalatable British cigarettes and very little chocolate or soap. Many of the old British *kriegies* regularly received nice parcels of cigarettes, food, and clothing from the United States through an organization called "Bundles for Britain," but it would be a long time before our pleas for winter clothing, American food items, American cigarettes, soap, and chocolate were answered.

The War Department, Departments of State and Commerce, and the American Red Cross were totally unprepared to activate a plan that would give the growing number of families of POWs a procedure for sending the things that were urgently needed. Carolyn and Beatrice Waters, the daughter of General Patton and wife of Army Lt. Col. John Waters, who had been captured at the Kasserine Pass disaster in North Africa, worked hard and long to get things started. Our mothers and wives were in the war, too. Carolyn kept a scrapbook that tells the story of her work to prod the government into organizing a program to expedite parcels destined for POWs. Her work also involved organizing and informing wives and mothers of ways to help their loved ones who were in the bag. Her scrapbook is now in the Air Force Academy Library. The work of wives and mothers in helping their POW sons, brothers, and husbands is a wonderful story waiting to be told.

We received some food, mostly dried fruits, from the Turkish Red Cross. We never saw eggs, of course, but one day our room acquired one fresh lemon. This was the only fresh fruit we saw for the entire war. We discussed how to use it and finally decided to give it to Bill Geiger since he looked like he might be coming down with tuberculosis. He ate it all, including the skin.

For Christmas 1942, I volunteered to make a fruit cake, and we all contributed our dried fruits, nuts, and sugar. From time to time the Turkish Red Cross sent us dates, raisins, dried persimmons, and nuts. By saving our meager rations we had enough for the cake. We ground up biscuits for the flour and used Dr. Lyons tooth powder for baking powder (it was largely baking soda). We had one small coal stove for all of the 180 of us in the block. The stove never got cold, but the oven seldom got hot enough to bake a cake. I had assumed the unwise responsibility of producing something good out of the savings of the entire room. The cake started to rise and then collapsed, but we ate it anyway and enjoyed it.

☆　☆　☆

Music provided an important cultural contribution to our otherwise sterile lives. We eventually formed fine orchestras and bands, as every camp had plenty of talented musicians and the International YMCA had been most effective in providing us with the necessary musical instruments. In addition, there were several phonograph machines in each camp, most of them privately owned but almost always available for general use. New records came in regularly and were avidly listened to by large groups. Sometime in late 1942 the Poles received a recording of *The Warsaw Concerto*. They were the logical ones to receive the record. It was the inspiring background music, by Addinsell, for a British film entitled *Dangerous Moonlight* about a Polish fighter pilot involved in the Battle of Britain. The Poles played it endlessly, and I became quite fond of it. To me it reflected most movingly the pathos of the Polish predicament in this war, especially the POWs who were now back in Poland, unable to communicate with the families they hadn't seen since the early days of the war. I told Carolyn about this in one of my letters and made the mistake of telling her to listen to it, as there was a message in it for her. She bought the record and spent hours trying to decipher the message, thinking that I had alluded to some coded message hidden in the music.

☆ ☆ ☆

In mid-November, Maj. Hal Houston came into the camp. He was a group intelligence officer and had "gone along for the ride" on a night raid in the aircraft of his group commander, Col. C. G. "Rojo" Goodrich of the 12th Bomb Group based in Egypt. They were shot down over Sidi Haunch near Benghazi that September night. What bitter irony. Houston had briefed the mission as a "milk run" (a mission with no expected enemy fire). After time in the hospital, Hal arrived in camp on 17 November. We roomed together for the remainder of our stay in the East Camp. Hal was a skilled administrative officer and was a great help to the adjutants for the rest of the war.

Rojo Goodrich, Houston's group commander, broke his back bailing out of the aircraft and was hospitalized in four different hospitals all the way from Africa to Germany. He finally arrived at Stalag Luft III from Oflag 64 (Shubin) along with a returning group of Brits who had left Stalag Luft III in the summer of 1942. As a full colonel, Goodrich automatically became the SAO when he arrived in the recently opened North Camp.

North Camp was the first of four new camps that would have to be built to cope with the ever increasing flow of new *kriegies*. It was located just west of the German garrison camp (or *lager*), a short walk on the east/west dirt road that bounded the camps to the north. As the day to move to the new North Camp approached, we convinced the Germans to allow us to go over to the new camp to start vegetable gardens and identify the best locations for the camp offices, medical clinic, and so forth. In addition, Bushell, Floody, and other key players on the X committee reconnoitered the new camp searching for good locations for future tunnels and factories. They also found and hid tools, bags of cement, and other items urgently needed for their activity. Most of the workers who built the camp were Russian POWs who didn't care, and for a few cigarettes, they were happy to help in this effort.

The X committee strategy was to start three tunnels at once before the ferrets had a chance to "memorize" the landscape of the camp. To detect clandestine operations, the ferrets depended heavily on noting changes in the surface soil, patterns of traffic, signs of activity under the huts, and so on. The opportunity to get three tunnels started, all in different locations and with different entrance systems, would possibly help us get the jump on the ferrets.

CHAPTER 7

North Camp

27 March to 8 September 1943

W e made the move to the new North Camp on a cold and windy day in March. The Germans searched us en route in the *Vorlager*, taking hours, but happily we lost very little of our escape gear. I ended the day with pneumonia and spent the next week in the camp hospital. I got a good rest, which was made memorable because I met an interesting RAF administrative officer who was also a patient.

In the grade of flight lieutenant, he had been captured after being badly wounded as a member of the British Expeditionary Forces in the Battle of France in 1940. He had been in POW hospitals ever since, suffering from a withered leg that should have been amputated. Designated a *grand blessé* (seriously wounded) under the rules of the Geneva Convention, he qualified for repatriation. In 1941 he'd been among the first group of British prisoners to board the famous hospital ship *Gripsholme*, destined for a mutual exchange with German POWs from England. These prisoners experienced the heartbreaking disappointment when the process was canceled because of an arbitrary last-minute issue introduced into the protocol by Hitler.

This officer, whose name I've regretfully long since lost, had been a sailor on a World War I British battleship that was sunk in the Dardenelles in an exchange of fire with a Turkish shore battery during the ill-fated Gallipoli campaign. Having survived this experience, he became a crewman on the HMS *Hardinge*, the supply ship for Lawrence of Arabia in the Red Sea in 1916 and 1917. I had lengthy conversations with this interesting man and found his positive attitude, after all he'd been through, to be very inspiring. He eventually was repatriated in a later, more successful exchange.

In the new North Camp we were initially given more space, and I chose an end room at the northwest corner of the camp in Block 105. All of the Americans were in this same general area. Many of the tall pine trees had been left standing in the camp on instructions of the commandant, and they helped soften the barren, gray ugliness inside the wire. The *Vorlager* had been extended across the north side of the camp, and we had a coal shed; a new, enlarged cooler; and a new, large sick bay to look at. Beyond this was another more heavily guarded outer wire with the ubiquitous goon boxes. On the east, west, and south we were surrounded by the pine forest, but this would not last long, as new camps were soon under construction adjacent to us to the south and west.

When Bushell arrived in the fall of 1942, both the commandant and the SBO cautioned Roger to relax and cease his efforts to escape, as the Gestapo would give him no mercy if he were caught. In spite of this, after the departure of Buckley, Roger assumed the job of controlling all the escape activity in the camp, and it was understood that he would continue in that role when we got the new North Camp.

He had asked me to take on the task of providing secure hiding places for our inventory of escape equipment. I became known as "Big S." We knew that in the spring when we moved to the new camp the Germans would search each of us thoroughly. The task of getting our money, false travel papers, tools, compasses, maps, and civilian clothing through the search would be a formidable one.

With that now all behind us we rapidly set to work organizing the escape effort including my job of protecting the three tunnel teams and the factories that had been set to work with a goal of equipping an estimated 200 escapees should we succeed in completing even one of the tunnels. This involved posting a duty officer to watch the gate at all times to ensure that we knew what Germans were in the camp. The ferrets would sometimes try hiding in an attic or under a hut to mess up the count so we would consider ourselves "goon-free" and expose some critical activity to discovery. We established zones throughout the camp within which certain factories operated, and every German in the camp was tailed so that these factories could quickly pack up in the event any German entered their zone. Each factory had its own watchers who were in touch with the overall warning system, and each could be packed up and converted to an innocuous activity in seconds. As clandestine work was continuous, it required shifts, and the total number of our men involved in security alone was several hundred. These men worked patiently, often wearily watching ferrets strolling around the camp but ready to give a signal, such as scratching their left ear, in the event a ferret got too close.

We hadn't been in the North Camp for more than a few days when a truly spectacular escape was attempted by an Australian named Johnny Stower. Without any assistance, he crossed the "dead line" opposite a goon box on the northwest side of camp and climbed over the fence under the goon box without being observed, then walked away. He made it all the way to the Swiss border, but was caught there and returned. It was a long hike through hostile country where everyone was alert to the appearance of strangers. Johnny was later lost during the tunnel escape in March of the next year.

Soon, three tunnels called Tom, Dick, and Harry were underway. Tom's trap was located in the hallway of the Polish block (123). An irregular hole was cut into a chimney pad, and using concrete earlier stolen from the workers who built North Camp, a new pad was poured. This pad did not bond to the edges of the hole—after hardening, it could be removed. When it was reinstalled, its edges were concealed by dust and dirt. The tunnel was to go straight out to the west, ending in the woods. Tom had the highest priority of the three tunnels, as there were rumors of a new camp to go up to the west of us.

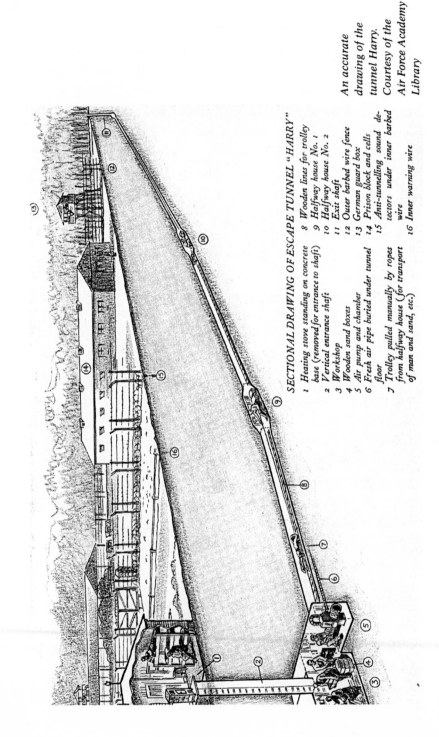

SECTIONAL DRAWING OF ESCAPE TUNNEL "HARRY"

1 Heating stove standing on concrete base (removed for entrance to shaft)
2 Vertical entrance shaft
3 Workshop
4 Wooden sand boxes
5 Air pump and chamber
6 Fresh air pipe buried under tunnel floor
7 Trolley pulled manually by ropes from halfway house (for transport of man and sand, etc.)
8 Wooden lines for trolley
9 Halfway house No. 1
10 Halfway house No. 2
11 Exit shaft
12 Outer barbed wire fence
13 German guard box
14 Prison block and cells
15 Anti-tunnelling sound detectors under inner barbed wire
16 Inner warning wire

An accurate drawing of the tunnel Harry. Courtesy of the Air Force Academy Library

Dick was entered through a trap under the large wooden grating in the center of the shower room in Block 122 and was intended to eventually tie into Tom. It was a clever trap, cut into the center of a concrete slab through which the drainage system had been diverted. It was a most implausible place for a tunnel to start. This tunnel ended up being converted to a large storage room. Dick was only made possible by the fact that the Germans had used an oversized drain large enough for a man to descend through.

Harry began under the concrete stove pad in the corner of a typical ten-man room on the west side of Block 104. The old pad was cut out and replaced by one that looked the same but was hinged at the back and could be lifted up when the stove was moved aside. Again, the contraband cement made this possible. Even the tile surface was replaced on the false slab. Harry was to go straight out to the north at a depth of thirty feet to defeat the seismographs the Germans had installed around the entire perimeter of the camp at a depth of about nine feet. The plan was for the tunnel to pass under the cooler, the outer north wire, and the dirt road, ending up in the woods. The tunnel would clearly have to be more than 300 feet long.

The exact distance was hard to measure. A team with surveying experience working from inside our camp attempted to triangulate the distance to the tree line beyond the road. In the end, however, as buildings blocked the view, their measurement came up short of the woods by about ten feet. This error would not be discovered until the night of the escape.

Harry was actually 330 feet long. Air at the face was supplied by a long pipe made from powdered-milk cans fastened together and buried in the tunnel. One man at the foot of the entrance shaft drew fresh air from a concealed inlet using a large bellows-type pump and pumped constantly when work was in progress. Electric lights were also strung along the tunnel, illuminating the face, the two resting stations along the way, and the work area at the foot of the entrance shaft. The wire was stolen from a careless worker, and electric power was tapped out of the wall of the hut where it could not be detected. This tunnel was a classic example of the state-of-the-art work achieved by determined men whose skill and experience was the result of four years of collective trial and error.

While all these intelligence-gathering and escape efforts proceeded, new *kriegies* arrived at an ever increasing rate. The British 1,000-bomber night operations were in full swing, creating havoc and great loss of life among civilians in cities all over Germany. Luftwaffe night fighters and flak were taking a heavy toll, and surviving bomber crews were rapidly filling up the old East Camp and the new North Camp. At the same time, the U.S. 8th Air Force daylight bombing campaign was approaching a critical stage, with heavy losses from enemy fighters as well as flak. The tactic of bombing exclusively military targets during daylight, without fighter support, had resulted in extensive losses, and few crews were completing their required fifty missions. The future of this concept was in doubt, and the survivors were rapidly filling the POW camps. As a result, the Germans found themselves building new camps around us as fast as they could.

It was in July, I believe, that the RAF hit Hamburg with a devastating raid that started a firestorm, destroying most of the city. I remember Roger Bushell reading in the Nazi Party newspaper, *The Volkischer Beobackter* (with which we were supplied daily in large quantities), that stern action would be taken against the citizens of Hamburg and that they would be deprived of ration cards if they did not return to the city. Apparently the people who were burned out of their homes and survived abandoned the area in such numbers that it caused an official reaction. Every day the papers had pages of death notices and obituaries. We knew then that Germany was being badly hurt by the RAF's 1,000-bomber raids.

We followed the course of the war with keen interest, listening to the German daily communiqués, which were piped in to us, and to the BBC, which we received through our secret radio. We also thoroughly debriefed new arrivals. I believe we were among the best-informed people in the war. The landing on Italian soil at Salerno in September 1943 was encouraging, but we knew that we wouldn't be liberated until the Allies landed in force somewhere on the west coast of Europe. We also knew that such a landing was not going to happen until the summer of 1944 at the earliest.

Several colonels and lieutenant colonels whom I knew came in during the spring and summer of 1943 and told

Maj. Jerry M. Sage, U.S. Army Special Forces, as he appeared in camp. Drawing by A. P. Clark

unusual survival stories. For example, there was Maj. Jerry Sage, Office of Strategic Services (OSS), who arrived on 21 April. He had been captured in Africa on 14 February while operating behind German lines. Somehow he managed to change his identity from that of a saboteur to that of a downed airman simply trying to make his way back to the American lines. Consequently he ended up in Stalag Luft III instead of being shot. Jerry was a blithe spirit— always jovial and upbeat, a great leader of young men, and a constant thorn in the side of the Germans. His escape attempts resulted in lots of time spent in the cooler, and eventually the commandant got rid of him by sending him, in June 1944, to Oflag 64 at Shubin. By then Oflag 64 had become the main camp for U.S. Army officers.

Jerry will always be remembered for the Fourth of July celebration that he organized and orchestrated that summer of 1943 in the North Camp. At unlock that morning, Jerry dressed as Uncle Sam and appeared leading a motley crew of all 600 Americans with the

Lt. Col. R. M. "Moose" Stillman.
Courtesy of the Air Force Academy
Library

Yankee Doodle trio: the fife, drum, and flag. We all paraded noisily through the British huts, waking the Brits up and making clear to them what the day meant to us. All day was spent in fun and games and consuming the horrible brews that had been carefully distilled for the occasion. Before the day was over, all of the senior officers were thrown into the fire pool (a pool of water saved for emergencies). Late in the afternoon, I happened to notice a body on the bottom of this shallow pool. How the man happened to be there nobody knew, but we dragged him out, pumped some water out of his lungs with artificial respiration, and he came to. As soon as he looked okay, the crowd lost interest in him and continued its raucous horseplay. The lad's name was Lester Kluever, and he'd only been in camp for a few weeks. I knew his big brother, who was also flying bombers over Europe. Lester was very lucky.

Lt. Col. R. M. "Moose" Stillman, whom I had known at West Point, also came in about the same time. He was the group commander of the first Martin Marauder group to arrive in England. He led their first bombing mission on 11 May 1943. It was a squadron effort flown at low level. They struck a power plant in Ijmuiden, Holland, and returned without loss. A few days later, to their disgust, they were sent back to repeat the mission, because for some reason the post-operation target photos showed little damage and few signs of bomb strikes in the target area. What they didn't know then was that they were bombing at such a low altitude that the British bomb fuses being used didn't have time to arm after release.

Moose also led the rerun on 17 May, and their mission orders required them to use essentially the same strike plan. This time the Germans were ready, and the whole squadron, except for one aircraft that aborted over the North Sea, was shot down. The tail was shot off Moose's aircraft as the formation hit the coast inbound. His wingmen watched the aircraft roll bottom up and crash in a fireball. When they arrived in camp, all of Moose's surviving squadron mates reported that he'd been killed. On 5 June, just two weeks later, Moose arrived. He had a broken little finger, two black eyes, and was sore all over. He had regained consciousness in a German hospital several days after the crash, and how he survived is known only to God.

Moose became my roommate, and we lived together until we moved out of the North Camp in October of 1943. I promptly wrote home and told Carolyn that Moose was here and was okay. I knew that his wife, "Noopie," was in San Antonio and that she and Carolyn had been friends for many years. Thus she was spared the long, agonizing wait to find out whether her Missing In Action (MIA) husband was alive or dead.

Lt. Col. Mel McNickle came in on 24 August. He was the commander of a P-47 Group and had been badly shot-up over Holland on 3 August. He had no memory of crash-landing in a short, muddy field, hitting some kind of obstruction, flipping upside down, and getting buried in the mud, unconscious. He was dug out by farmers, and when he arrived in camp three weeks later he was in severe pain from injuries to his neck and shoulders and was covered with shrapnel wounds. He had an identical twin brother named Marv. The three of us had gone through flying school together and flew together in the First Pursuit Group at Selfridge Field until the war. Marv was with me in the 31st and was flying on the same mission when I was shot down. They both later became general officers, and our paths continued to cross all through our service careers.

Also on 24 August, Col. Delmar Spivey came in. He was the second full colonel to join us and was a West Point classmate of

*Lt. Col. M. F. "Mel" McNickle.
Courtesy of the Air Force Academy
Library*

*Col. Delmar T. Spivey. Courtesy of
the Air Force Academy Library*

Rojo Goodrich. He had been selected by General Henry Arnold to command a new stateside school that was being established to train aerial gunners so that they might actually score hits on the German fighters who were attacking our bombers with such devastating success. The claims by these gunners were known to be highly exaggerated, and a lot of their shooting was just a waste of ammunition. Arnold told Spivey, along with the three or four other senior officers who were to join him in running this new school, to go over and fly some missions before starting the training. This they did, and, I believe, all were shot down. They all joined Spivey at Stalag Luft III including Col. Bill Kennedy, Col. A. Y. Smith, and Col. Danny Jenkins. This must have given General Arnold, the chief of the Army Air Forces, a sobering message. Del Spivey was actually manning the tail gun in his aircraft when it went down. He was a first-rate man and shortly became the SAO of the new all-American Center Camp, which was about to be established in the former NCO camp.

Sometime in April of 1943, Rojo Goodrich had arrived. He came in with Wings Day from Oflag 64 at Shubin. Shortly thereafter, Group Captain Massey went off to a German hospital for treatment for his game leg. Rojo thus became the senior officer in the North Camp. Wings Day was a decorated veteran of the First World War, but through the misfortunes of war, he still held the rank corresponding to our lieutenant colonel. I'm sure he was quite content to be unburdened of the responsibility of being the camp's senior officer. Wings laid on a special ceremony for this so-called change of command. He instructed all of us to wear our proper uniforms, in so far as we could, to the morning appel (roll

Col. C. G. "Rojo" Goodrich. Courtesy of the Air Force Academy Library

call), and he held the assembled *kriegies* in place after the German count had been completed. He made a brief speech announcing that he was turning over command and praised Rojo in a typically smart British manner. He then turned to Rojo, saluted him smartly, and indicated that it was his turn to say something. Rojo faced the troops, paused for a long moment, and then said, "Well, here I am and there you are. Dismissed."

☆ ☆ ☆

One day during the early summer, the commandant brought a senior German army officer to the camp to show him around. They came in through the gate in a small sports car with an enlisted driver and parked near the first block. The two officers strolled slowly around the circuit while the commandant showed his guest the wire, lights, guard towers, dead line, and so on. Von Lindeiner was quite proud of Stalag Luft III, for in spite of our escape activity, he apparently felt that he had one of the most escape-proof camps in Germany. The group had left the young driver to guard the car, which promptly drew a crowd. While the driver was engaged in conversation with his back to the car, someone filched a book that was seen lying on the seat. The book was quickly spirited away, and it turned out to be a listing of the hundreds of wanted military criminals in the various German armed forces. The commandant and his guest returned and departed the camp without noticing the loss of the book.

It wasn't long, however, before Sergeant Glemnitz came in looking very stern and agitated. He went straight to the SBO and reported the loss which, of course, had been duly reported to him. The SBO expressed surprise and promised to see what he could do to find the book and get it returned. Meanwhile, the book was passed to Tim Walenn, the head of the forgery department, and was inscribed on the frontispiece with a neatly printed statement to the effect that the book had been examined by the POWs in Stalag Luft III; it was then dated and stamped. The next day Glemnitz came in to see Wings Day with a bottle of wine and appealed again for the return of the book before something very terrible happened to the whole camp. Wings was expecting him and returned the book forthwith and, I understand, popped the cork for a brief toast with Glemnitz.

☆ ☆ ☆

My job as "Big S" was going okay, and the tunneling was proceeding, although under increasing scrutiny from the Germans. In my spare time I had started a collection of clippings from the German newspapers and magazines that were sent into the camp in copious quantities. I had started in the East Camp with photographs of Hitler and all of the key figures in the German government. This was soon followed by an effort to obtain photos of all of the German army, navy, and Luftwaffe generals and other national heroes. I soon had most of the outstanding pilots—some with more than a hundred victories. Then the collection inexorably broadened to include clippings of all of the German weapons, from the smallest to the largest, and all of the aircraft. The collection was being mounted in big scrapbooks, the covers made out of cardboard from the Red Cross parcels and the pages from the newspapers. It was beginning to become more than a hobby, almost an obsession, and it contained a wealth of information that I had vague hopes of someday getting home.

By this time I was getting mail from my father and my sister, Mary. The mail from my father, who was a colonel in the Army Medical Corps and commanded a huge general hospital in Walla Walla, Washington, was filled with instructions on how to survive. He was especially interested in our nutrition, which was his hobby. He started sending me boxes of vitamin pills in Carolyn's parcels, and I soon had enough to feed my friends as well. I was a little irked that Dad seldom gave me news of family but rather provided instruction on how to get my iron from rusty nails and reminders that dandelion greens were very nutritious. Later, at Moosburg, we actually did harvest dandelions that were growing in the barbed-wire areas, but at Stalag Luft III this would have drawn fire.

I was growing very uneasy as Carolyn, despite repeated requests, had sent me no pictures of herself or the children. I was having trouble remembering what they looked like and had begun to wonder whether she had a reason for not sending a picture. Was there a problem with one of the kids? Had she put on a lot of weight? But finally, a lovely photo arrived. She was as beautiful as ever, and the kids looked fine, but of course, were a lot older. This photo was a great comfort to me.

☆ ☆ ☆

I was one of the senior officers among the Americans, and as the oldest *kriegie* I was approachable. Many of the young first and second lieutenants came to me with problems or unusual stories. I enjoyed this status immensely. Often new men came in with strange and unusual stories and I made a point of learning about them. We had at least two intelligence officers, nonpilots who had gone along for the ride. Maj. Hal Houston was one and Capt. Bill "Pop" Cody was another. Pop had been in the nose of an RP-38 reconnaissance aircraft, was shot in the face, and spent three days in a dinghy out in the Mediterranean Sea. I believe he was the oldest American *kriegie* in camp; he was born in 1904. There were many navigators, of course. One was a major who had been shot down in January 1942. I say shot down, although his B-17 and the rest of the crew got home. He thought he had heard someone shout "bail out," and he did. Imagine the heartache he had to live with.

There also were lots of pilots who lived with the guilt that came from believing that their mistakes had caused them and their crews (in the case of the bombers) to be lost to the war effort. Some needed counseling, and there were several suicides, but, to my knowledge, no Americans took their own lives. One Brit came to see me in tears, agonizing unnecessarily over his mishap, and I tried to reassure him. He was a Baufighter pilot whose lonely and dangerous job was to fly from England to Malta once a week at night, high over enemy-held France, carrying dispatches. He had lost control of his aircraft in a thunderstorm and had to bail out. He feared that his dispatches had fallen into enemy hands. I did what I could to reassure him.

☆   ☆   ☆

From my little room up in the northwest corner of the camp (number 106) I could see out on our small world. There wasn't much to see, but anything outside the wire was interesting. For example, there was the Russian POW who spent the summer cracking rocks for a hardstand. He labored near the coal shed in the *Vorlager*, right in front of me. From time to time, I threw him a pack of cigarettes over the wire. For him, American cigarettes were pure gold if he could avoid getting stripped of them by the guards before he got back to his camp.

I also noticed a small monument in the edge of the woods to my left, on the south side of the road that bound the north side of the entire camp. It was made of stone and stood about six feet tall. I managed to get a friendly German to go and write down for me the inscription on the monument.

On one side in French it read:

À la mémoire
des soldats Français
morts en terre Allemande
ce monument est pieusement érigé
par le petit fils de Marichalde de Castellane
Comte Boniface de Hatzfeldt

This roughly translates to:

In memory
of French soldiers
who perished in Germany
this monument is reverently erected
by the grandson of Marshal de Castellane
Count Boniface of Hatzfeldt

On the other side it read in German:

Den hier aux dem ruckzuge
aus Russland am nervenfieber
gesturbenen soldaten den
grossen Napolionischer Armee
in frommer Erinnerung gewidnet

Which translates to:

Dedicated in devout memory
to those soldiers
of the Great Napoleonic Army
who died here of
typhoid fever
on the retreat from Russia.
May the passer-by
pray for you.

☆   ☆   ☆

The little monument along the road north of camp dedicated to casualties from Napoleon's Army during the retreat from Russia. Drawing by A. P. Clark

When the new South Camp was nearing completion in July 1943, we thought it might be possible to do a walk out with a small party of senior officers under escort, ostensibly to check on arrangements for essential functions in the new American camp. Bob Van-DerStok was eager and fully qualified to be the German escort. He was to be fitted out with a homemade *Feldwebel* uniform. Both Rojo and I wanted to try it, and Stanford Tuck and Bill Jennings, the adjutant, made up our group of four. We made a plausible-looking party, and Roger Bushell, reflecting his remarkable genius for such adventures, laid our little show on in conjunction with a larger escape, which we were to immediately follow.

Rojo and I planned to travel separately. I was going to France as a French worker returning home on leave. I spoke a little French, but it was a long way for someone who spoke hardly any German and would have to travel on foot. Still, I thought, "What the hell, here is a chance." While it was a long shot, it was also a break in the deadly routine of the camp. I owned a jacket that had been sent to me by friends. Glemnitz was suspicious when I first received it, saying that it was too civilian looking, which it was, but I talked him into letting me keep it. I wore my "pink" uniform trousers (the nickname for dress trousers) and a billed cap that looked German. I would carry a forged leave letter, supposedly sent from a large nearby firm that we knew employed French laborers, along with a simple ID without photo. Money, maps, compass, and lots of concentrated rations were all carefully sewn inside my jacket.

The other group involved about thirty *kriegies* scheduled to be escorted out the gate and down the road a short distance to have their clothing and bedding fumigated in the German *Vorlager*. Their block had become infested with bedbugs, and these fumigation parties had been going out daily under escort by two German corporals. It had become routine. In this instance, the two German escorts were sidetracked by conversation, irresistible hot chocolate, and real cigarettes. In the meantime, a similar group, carrying stuff that looked like bedding but which covered up their escape kits, approached the gate under escort of our two phony goons, who were wearing excellent homemade uniforms. They marched on out the gate unchallenged and turned right down the road toward the German *Vorlager*.

Our small group then assembled casually at the first gate, and Bob VanDerStok showed his pass to the guard without any challenge. As we went out we could see, out of the corner of our eyes, these thirty *kriegies* running into the woods, throwing their false bedding over their shoulders, and disappearing, completely unobserved by the Germans. It was hard to keep from laughing. There was a problem at the second gate with Bob's papers, and the Germans went into their typical shouting act and called out the guard. We had successfully passed the first gate, but it turned out a new mark that our forgers did not know about had been added to the back of the gate pass. So off to the cooler we went for a two-week stint. This time when Glemnitz took my jacket he was not amused, and I never saw it again.

Eventually all thirty escapees in the delousing party were rounded up, so the cooler became quite crowded, and we were two and three to a room. Rojo and I shared a bunk, and I was in the top rack. I finished reading *The Life of Leonardo Da Vinci* and slept a lot. Rojo was great on ribald limericks. With the stub of a pencil, I carefully wrote down on the ceiling of the cell—which was close above my head—all of the limericks he could remember, with illustrations. In a cell down the hall from us was a Russian fighter pilot awaiting a death sentence. He had been a P-39 pilot and apparently had hit a guard over the head in an escape attempt. He had drawn a beautiful picture of the P-39 aircraft covering his wall. We would get a glimpse of his work when we were escorted to and from the abort (latrine).

From the small abort window I could see out of the compound and down the dirt road that bordered the north face of the camp. I will never forget the night just at dusk when, as I gazed longingly out this window, I saw a lovely young woman wearing a white turtleneck sweater. She was waiting under the lamppost for her German soldier. I have always been sure that she was "Lilli Marlene." A wave of longing swept over me as I thought of home and my own lovely wife and three children. How could I have possibly gotten myself into such a mess? I wondered. And would it ever be over? Would I ever see my loved ones again?

Shortly before my escape attempt, Jerry Sage had managed to slip out of an ambulance taking him into town for an X-ray for suspected broken ribs from a rugby game. He was able to clear the area and walked about 130 miles—almost to the Czechoslovakian border—before he was caught. He was back in the crowded cooler just as Rojo and I came out.

Jerry was a professional troublemaker when it came to harassing the goons. He was in a three-man cell and made a big fuss to get something to eat when he was returned, ravenous from his escapade. Eventually, late that night, the row brought the commandant to the cell, and when the guards shouted at Jerry to stand up, he sat where he was, putting on his slippers. Von Lindeiner drew his pistol in a towering rage that caused Jerry's two roommates to hit the floor as Jerry slowly stood up. Jerry was a very cool customer. He could see that the commandant was shaking with rage and might shoot. He quietly cautioned Von Lindeiner to be reasonable and reminded him that he was a gentleman and could not shoot him under the rules of the Geneva Convention. The commandant told Jerry that *he* was certainly not a gentleman, but a wolf, and he would be taught discipline. This was a close one, and thereafter Jerry was a marked man. His actions were consistent with his special-forces training. He was skilled at the techniques of silent death and was a very tough warrior. Eventually the commandant got rid of him by sending him to the U.S. Army officers' camp at Shubin, Oflag 64, where he should have been all along.

There were two other interesting escapes at this time that showed the problems the commandant faced and which, we suspected, were causing him trouble with Himmler and his Gestapo thugs. The Gestapo reportedly told him that if he couldn't keep us in, they would show him how to do it.

The first was Sammy Vogle's escape. He was an American fighter pilot captured in Africa. He and a colleague managed to hide in a trash wagon, and he avoided the probing of the ferrets at the gate while his buddy was found and pulled out. In due course, Sammy jumped out, but he was seen by the old German driver of the horse and wagon, so he didn't have much of a head start. However, he made it on foot all of the way into Czechoslovakia. Unfortunately, when Sammy sought help from a Czech, he was turned in and ended up in the cooler too. He was gone for several weeks, and we had begun to hope he had made it.

Alvin "Sammy" Vogle. This photograph was made in camp in an effort to produce a satisfactory passport photo. It was not satisfactory.

The other escape about that time was made by two Brits, Welch and Morrison. They went out on the delousing parade and planned to steal an aircraft from the Kuepher Airfield, which was just northeast of Sagan. They wore blue homemade Luftwaffe overalls and caps with the appropriate insignia. They reached the airfield, climbed into a small twin-engine plane, and got one engine started. They had trouble with the other engine, and about that time a couple of German pilots arrived to take the aircraft. Welch and Morrison succeeded in convincing these pilots that they were simply readying the aircraft for them, and they got away with it. Unfortunately, they were caught as they tried to get away with a second plane. So they ended up in the cooler too. It was a busy summer from the escape point of view, and the poor commandant was a very unhappy man.

During this summer I also picked up a German contact, Feldwebel Von Gutenberg. I don't remember how it started, but he was obviously authorized to come visit with me and I was authorized by Rojo to visit with him. He spoke good English, was well educated, and I believe he was from an old aristocratic family. At war's end he wrote to me that all of the displaced members of his family were living, very crowded, in a small family castle. I tried to help him with food parcels, and the last time I heard from him he was selling cars in Detroit.

Feldwebel Von Gutenberg. Photograph taken after the war by Von Gutenberg.

Our chats were interesting and, insofar as he felt safe to do so, he confided his doubts about the war. I didn't learn much from him, and I don't think he learned anything from me that could have affected the camp. On Easter Sunday 1943, he brought me one egg. I arranged for an announcement to be made at appel that immediately after dismissal there would be an Easter egg hunt among the trees near my block. That morning I had made arrangements to be counted in my room and hid the egg near one of the trees while all others were standing appel. It wasn't long before the thundering herd arrived, and the egg was found, fried, and devoured within minutes.

☆   ☆   ☆

The Brits also controlled contacts with the Germans. This was done in order to use these contacts solely as a means of obtaining needed information and to prevent leaks through careless conversation, though the average *kriegie*'s knowledge was quite limited concerning what was sensitive about our activities and about the information needed back in England. Some of the Brits' efforts were quite sophisticated. For example, Wings Day, as an old prisoner, had been in at least five different camps and had made many contacts with Luftwaffe officers. Some of these officers greatly respected Wings, and from time to time, one or two of them would even come to see him. In particular, there also was a German *Lager* officer who, presumably with the commandant's approval, came in to chat with Wings. He talked too much, and one time let the cat out of the bag about forthcoming new weapons. In *Wings Day*, author Sydney Smith says that this officer talked about new rocket weapons with which Hitler would soon end the war. From another contact it was learned that Peenemunde was an experimental base filled with scientists working on rockets. This type of intelligence was big stuff and, when sent home through the code system, was very well received.

☆   ☆   ☆

During the summer of 1943, the number of American *kriegies* continued to grow and the Brits were faced with an adjustment. Many of the young American *kriegies* were boisterous and loudmouthed, and many used profanity freely. The Brits complained about the

German ferret demonstrating use of sandbags under his coat for distributing sand. German photograph, courtesy of the Air Force Academy Library

bad habit of some who spat, even on the circuit path, when they could just as well have spat over the dead line rail along which they walked. We had some kids who had not finished high school, and many had had questionable home training. But they could fight, and that was what it was all about at that point. Because of the crowding and discontent at North Camp, most Americans, including me, were eager to get into our own camp.

By August the Germans were convinced that tunneling was going on in the North Camp. They cut down all of the lovely pine trees that the commandant had allowed to remain in the camp, claiming that they interfered with the ferrets' endless nervous efforts to discover where the sand was coming from.

Glemnitz built a tree stand in the woods west of the camp, and the ferrets could be seen concealed behind the foliage with a big telescope, observing our every move for hours at a time.

We had great difficulty disposing of the sand coming out of three tunnels. We buried it in the gardens, the walls and ceilings of the huts, and, finally, created a dumping ground in an area where strenuous athletic activity had deliberately torn up the dark forest floor to reveal yellow sand. The "penguins" casually brought the sand out of the buildings stowed in bags inside their trousers or under their overcoats, and they loosened tie strings to slowly distribute the sand into this area and push it around with their feet while watching some athletic activity. I believe we raised the level

German ferret with sand cart used in tunnel Harry. Photograph obtained from the Germans after the war. Courtesy of the Air Force Academy Library

of that sports area by a foot. By the time it was completed, Harry alone had required about fifty-two cubic yards of sand to be moved surreptitiously out of Block 104.

Work was stopped on Dick when little more than a good-sized room was created under the shower floor, and Tom was given first priority for two reasons: we Americans were about to be moved to South Camp, which was nearing completion just beyond the south fence, and many of us had earned a crack at going out. Roger Bushell felt we deserved the chance. Also, the Germans were beginning to cut trees to the west of us for another new camp. Tom was to surface just inside this tree line. So it became a race against time.

Right in the middle of this critical period we received a message from British intelligence telling us that a V-1 rocket assembly plant was believed to be located somewhere near our camp, and we were asked to try to find it. The V-1s had not yet been launched against London, but their existence was known to the Brits. Those of us who were competing for a place on the tunnel list were required to agree to direct our travel after escape to a designated compass direction until we were either caught or clear of the area (meaning about fifty miles). Thus it was hoped that someone would find the rocket plant and it would then be reported home one way or another. I recall that we were all volunteers for the task even though, in some cases, we were asked to depart from our escape plan and undertake what was clearly espionage. We felt good about being needed in the war effort.

Unfortunately, Tom was discovered in early September through sheer chance. A ferret, killing time in the hallway of the Polish block, was doodling with his ramrod in the dust of the concrete floor when he noticed the dust-filled outline of the trap lid. The tunnel had already reached the edge of the trees and was complete except for the exit shaft. The Germans blew the tunnel up with such vigor that they collapsed the roof of the Polish block.

On 8 September 1943, all of the Americans departed either for South Camp or Center Camp. We had entered the North Camp in March with fewer than 200 Americans, and when we left in September of that year there were about 2,000 Americans. About 800 went to Center Camp with Colonel Spivey as the SAO, and 1,200 went to the South Camp with SAO Colonel Goodrich.

CHAPTER 8

South Camp

8 September 1943 to 27 January 1945

I t wasn't a very long walk to South Camp, as the Germans had put the gate in the northeast corner, which led into the woods in the German garrison's enclave. Since the gate opened into woods, it became attractive from an escape point of view. After one daylight attempt by a too-eager *kriegie* who attempted to crawl under the gate, it was moved to the west side, exiting into a long north-south alley shared by the West Camp, which was still under construction. We were searched on our way into the new camp, but I don't recall that it was very meticulous, and we managed to get

South Camp senior American officer and his staff including fifteen block commanders. From left to right, back row: Fleming, Beckham, Mills, unidentified, Diamond, Adamina, Williams, unidentified, Landford, D. M. Jones, Ferguson, Aldridge. Middle row: McNickle, Klocko, Clark, Miller, Goodrich, Parker, Smart, C. D. Jones, Stillman. Bottom row: Williamson, Schrupp, Widen, Burden, MacDonald, Schuck, Embach, Griffin. German photograph, courtesy of the Air Force Academy Library

South Camp kriegies *on appel. German photograph, courtesy of the Air Force Academy Libary*

enough contraband through to make a good start on our own escape program.

South Camp functioned well right from the start, as all staff activities were conducted by men who had been working with the Brits and were eager to get going on their own. Rojo Goodrich took control in a positive manner and was stern and unyielding with the Germans. Mel McNickle was the adjutant and did a fine job. Dave Pollak took over the parcels job and thereafter spent most of his days in the warehouse in the *Vorlager* managing this important task. Dave was from a prominent family in Cincinnati, and after the war he hosted the first few reunions. He was highly respected and well liked by all former *kriegies*. Jack Shuck took over the kitchen and was a dedicated worker there for the next year and a half. Rojo asked me to handle the escape business, and I had plenty of enthusiastic help. Rojo had fifty-eight men on the camp staff. Fifteen of them were the block commanders, and they were very important in maintaining the discipline and morale of the men in camp. They were captains and majors, and they did a great job all the way up until our liberation in Bavaria in April 1945. The jobs assigned to the balance of this group ranged from mail officer to the physiotherapy and laundry officers. They were all glad to have something to do, and they made the camp run like a military outfit.

One important personality who chose to join us in South Camp as chaplain was Murdo Ewan MacDonald. Padre Mac, as

he was called, had been an ordained minister, Church of Scotland, before the war, but he volunteered to join a Scottish regiment and trained as a parachutist. He had been a well-known boxer as a young man, so he was back in his element. His regiment was sent to North Africa, and he engaged in dangerous parachute insertions to cause trouble behind the German lines. On one of these, he was captured and managed to conceal his undercover identity so he was not unceremoniously shot. He had joined three or four Americans, also shot down, who were attempting to return to Allied lines. They briefed him to talk and act like an airman, and he was sent to Stalag Luft III.

Padre Mac was very popular in our camp, and his inspiring sermons delivered in a strong Scottish brogue caused men to fight for a seat in church on Sundays. After the war he and his American wife faithfully attended all of our reunions

On the right is "Padre" Murdo MacDonald with Captain Brown of Center Camp. This photo was taken at Moosburg after liberation. Brown caught the fish in the nearby Iser River. Courtesy of the Air Force Academy Library

and traditionally spoke at the closing breakfast. All of us were very fond of him.

Soon after our arrival in South Camp, Lt. Ewell McCright reported to me at the urging of his roommates. They told me he needed a job badly, as he was going stir crazy. I happened to have one that I'd been handling myself since the first Americans started arriving. Now I saw an opportunity to get needed help. The job involved keeping a record of each American *kriegie* in camp. I had established a brief format that included all of the information that we could safely keep, i.e. name, rank, serial number; home address; age; blood type; religion; where, when, and how shot down and captured; combat wound, if any; dates and camps in which detained; and *kriegie* number. I had kept the record in a small notebook that I naively thought would last me until the end of the war.

McCright eagerly accepted the job and needed no urging or further guidance. By the time we were evacuated from Sagan in January 1945, he had interviewed all 2,200 men in South Camp. He filled three large ledger books with meticulous, neatly printed entries and later carried these heavy volumes on our forced march to Bavaria, finally getting them home after the war. He then donated them to the National Archives, where they have since become a very valuable source of information on the former South Camp *kriegies*. I doubt that any other air forces camp brought home such valuable and historical information. Arnold Wright, a war history buff from Benton, Arkansas, carefully transcribed and edited this mass of information and made it the centerpiece of a book about South Camp of Stalag Luft III, *Behind the Wire: Stalag Luft III South Compound*, which he published in 1994. This book quickly sold out two editions, has brought many lost friends together, and assisted former *kriegies* in establishing veterans' claims for war-related injuries. It also served many other useful purposes, including earning the late Ewell McCright a well-earned place in the Arkansas Hall of Patriots.

Dick Kimball's book, *Clipped Wings*, which was published in 1948, is another remarkable book about South Camp. It tells a very accurate story and contains excellent photographs, some of which were secretly taken with the cameras we received from U.S. Army Intelligence. These cameras were shipped to us in special parcels that appeared to have come from families but were actually sent by an army intelligence agency. Each parcel's outer cover included a secret mark so we could identify it and discreetly smuggle it past the goons in the parcels warehouse. Dick

Second Lt. Ewell R. McCright. This photograph was taken on 22 January 1944, the day before he was shot down. Courtesy of the McCright family

Kimball's book sold out in two editions and is now a valuable collector's item.

My objective in the use of our secret cameras was to photograph all of the essential elements of our life in prison camp including German personalities, the security facilities, the rations, the living conditions, and so forth. I knew it would be quite a coup and would provide important informal history of the camp if we were able to get all these photos home. None of the photos were developed at the camp, they were hidden carefully and brought home after the war. All except those taken by one of my photographers (who kept his and copyrighted them for his own use) were turned in to our intelligence office. This vital work was conducted at considerable risk, as most of it could be considered espionage.

When we departed North Camp, Roger Bushell shut down tunneling activity to take the pressure off of Block 104 and the Harry tunnel. At this same time, the German security people appeared to be concentrating an undue amount of attention on South Camp, and I was surprised. I could never prove it, but I believe Roger allowed the word to leak out to the goons that the big tunnelers were the Americans, and now that Tom had been found and the Americans were gone, the Brits were in deep trouble with no skilled tunnelers. Sergeant Glemnitz started spending all of his time in our new camp with some of his sharpest ferrets, and we couldn't get anything going.

On 8 November 1943, the Germans assigned a goon to shadow me everywhere I went from unlock in the morning until lockup at night. He had orders never to let me out of his sight. This went on for several weeks, and Glemnitz was embarrassed and made it clear to me that it was the commandant's idea and not his. I could easily lose my shadow and did so a few times by suddenly jumping out a window and getting lost in the crowd, to illustrate that this method of keeping me out of mischief was not effective. To add to Glemnitz's troubles, about fifty *kriegies* started following him around one day in a long tail, which they dubbed a conga line. He lost his cool and started to draw his pistol when they bumped into him, making it clear that it wasn't to happen again, and it didn't. A few days later my tail was discontinued.

☆   ☆   ☆

Our own orchestra and band were soon organized and led by Maj. Hal Diamond, who had previous big-time band experience. His group was well equipped, thanks to the YMCA, and he had some very talented musicians such as Dusty Runner, who was real hot with the trumpet. From time to time the band was permitted to visit and play in the other compounds. One day in late November 1943, Dusty and his jazz band were being escorted back to our camp from the North Camp where they had been playing. The Brits there were in formation on the sports field, being counted by the goons. The band was outside the wire but within earshot of the Brits on parade. They paused and struck up *God Save the King* and every Brit immediately faced the music at stiff attention, saluting. The Germans were not amused. For punishment there were no more intercamp band visits, and the band was silenced for a month. This was typical of the Germans. The commandant gave privileges to try to create a happy camp with no escape activity, and then there would be an incident of some sort generating a heavy-handed reaction dictated by the security staff.

☆ ☆ ☆

Since the beginning of the war, the British POWs had enjoyed the services of enlisted prisoners whom they called "batmen." This is an interesting reflection on the prewar social status of the officer corps of the RAF. These batmen brought them tea the first thing in the morning, prepared their meals, hauled hot water, handled the trash and garbage for the entire compound, and did other common chores. As the war started bringing in wartime officers of a generally lower status and in large numbers, this batman policy had to be modified. Their work became limited to compound-wide chores. When we were separated from the Brits, the Germans brought in U.S. Army privates to do such work in our compound. They were not volunteers, and their performance was not very

The "Luft Bandsters," our talented band/orchestra. German photograph, courtesy of the Air Force Academy Library

satisfactory. Later we were able to replace them with volunteers from among our NCO crewmen, and the arrangement worked fine. These men did the common compound chores and lived and ate as we did. They were much better off with us.

In mid-October of 1943, *kriegies* from Italy began arriving. They had been held by the Italians in large camps much like ours. When Italy capitulated on 8 September, the POWs were faced with a dilemma: should they run off when the Italian guards departed or stay put as they were directed by their SAOs, who expected prompt Allied recovery efforts? They chose to stay, and when they awoke the next morning, the Germans were manning the gates and guard towers. The prisoners were promptly locked in crowded boxcars and shipped off to camps in Germany. They arrived in wretched condition, as they were frequently bombed, resulting in casualties. Some of them did manage to escape en route.

Also in October 1943, several of our severely wounded were repatriated. I briefed two who looked like they would keep their mouths shut and report accurately to authorities when debriefed back in the States. I told them of our clandestine work, what kind of materials we needed, and I gave them undeveloped photographs of the camp area. These photographs showed the German defensive positions being constructed around the camp. These items were carefully embedded in their crutches and other prostheses, and I learned after the war that these men had faithfully reported as requested.

✫ ✫ ✫

Christmas Eve was always a poignant time for us. We were not locked up until about midnight, and there was carol singing around the camp and lots of *kriegies* visiting around. On Christmas morning 1943, Rojo visited the theater and wished the assembled *kriegies* a good Christmas, predicting a better one next year. This was one of his rare public utterances.

That night, well before dark, a strange thing happened. A couple of *kriegies* who had probably imbibed a little too much hooch began to climb the wire that separated us from the North Camp. This was the standard eight-foot-high double fence with concertina wire coiled in between. The goon boxes were at both ends of this fence. Oddly, there were no shots fired, and other *kriegies* soon followed. They were going over to wish their old British friends a Merry Christmas! Soon some Brits showed up at the wire and climbed over into our camp. It was dark by that time, and the goons came to life and fired a burst over their heads. That

Col. John Stevenson, who later retired as a major general. Official Air Force photograph

cleared the wire in a hurry. I recall the tinkling of the several tin cups that were abandoned hanging in the wire. The next day we had a long morning appel in both camps, and the thirteen Yanks and four Brits were escorted back to their proper camps with a stern warning. They were all very lucky not to have been shot while in the wire.

On 29 December 1943, we had our first shooting in the camp. Col. John Stevenson, who had been shot down in Italy and arrived in camp in September 1943, was shot through both legs above the knee as he was playing bridge by candlelight in his room during a night air raid. The guard whose shot entered the barracks claimed he thought he saw a running figure. Stevenson's injury in one leg was severe, and the Germans sent him off to a proper hospital where they did bone surgery, but he was permanently crippled.

On New Year's Day 1944, I called a meeting of my people: all those who were running the factories, providing the security for all this work, working with the goons to obtain specific information or equipment, and our radio operators and helpers. It was a group of about thirty men. We were not having much success, and we were all a little disheartened. I gave them a little pep talk to encourage them and impress on them that what we were doing was worth the effort so they shouldn't be discouraged.

My security man was Ed Sconiers. He had a tough job, as the ferrets were giving us a bad time. They were everywhere, so we had difficulty getting a tunnel started and keeping the factories going. We lost some important stuff. I didn't think Ed looked very well, and he complained of an earache. I thought nothing more of it until a few days later when his roommates reported that he was out of his mind and needed to be restrained. There was no way for us to handle such cases, and we had to turn Ed over to the doctor in the camp lazarette (hospital). He was promptly sent off to the German hospital at Lublin, a town some distance to the east of Sagan, where he died on 23 January 1944. The Germans said that he died of heart failure, but I have always believed they handled him the same way they handled their own insanity cases. I think they simply disposed of him.

Padre MacDonald, Rojo Goodrich, Mel McNickle, Dick Klocko, and I were escorted on parole to the city of Lublin to bury

Burial of Ed Sconiers in Lublin. German photograph, courtesy of the Air Force Academy Library

Ed. It was a sad but very interesting experience for us to get out of
the camp for a day, and I have many vivid memories of the trip. We
traveled to Lublin by local train, a journey of about two hours, and
en route we passed a large forested area that had been burned out.
Prisoners in striped suits were working there, and I recalled the
towering firestorm cloud that hung over the area the previous
summer. We also passed a Luftwaffe twin-engine flight training
school with a crowded circuit of aircraft apparently in a landing
pattern. My eyes were hungry for such sights after eighteen
months behind the wire. We were held in a comfortable prewar
German army barracks for several hours before being walked to
the city cemetery. From the barracks window I watched a formal
guard mount and was impressed with the appearance and marching skill of the soldiers. They passed in review marching in
Achtung strickte (goose step).

The cemetery was a typical urban facility with an imposing iron
gate and fence, lots of ivy, neat stone monuments, and tidy gravel
paths. The casket was wheeled out on a large cart, and I was surprised that it was a very fancy ornamented metal affair. We made a
bad decision when several of us shouldered the casket and walked
off with it before we knew how far we were going. The casket was
as heavy as lead, and before long we were rotating the task among
the five of us, getting thoroughly worn out.

We were led through the cemetery to a back lot near a railroad
track on which stood a stationary line of boxcars filled with young
German soldiers who were quietly watching us. A newly dug grave
awaited among several others marked by flimsy wooden crosses.
We put our massive casket down, removed from it a plain wooden
one, and prepared to lower it into the grave with handheld straps.
We had placed a very plain hand-painted American flag, supplied
by the Germans, on the casket before lowering it, but failed to perform the proper ritual of removing and folding the flag before the
box was in the ground. I cringed when a German soldier jumped
down into the grave onto the flag with his muddy boots and

retrieved it. There were no honors or firing squad, and I think poor old Sconiers is still there, probably in an unmarked grave, since Lublin was behind the Iron Curtain for many years. I felt very bad about this bumbling burial ceremony, but we had little experience in military funerals so we were all ill-prepared for it.

Ed Sconiers wore the Distinguished Flying Cross, which, I believe, was the first one to be awarded in the European theater of operations. Ed was a bombardier, as he had washed out of flying school because he had trouble landing an aircraft. Flying out of England on one of his early missions, Ed's aircraft was badly shot up, the pilot was killed, and the copilot was severely wounded. Ed brought the B-17 back and landed it safely. I have always felt terrible about what happened to him, and I wondered if my pep talk might have been too much for him in his weakened condition. He was married, and his wife lived in Defuniak Springs, Florida. After the war I tried to visit her but was unable to find her.

☆   ☆   ☆

In January of 1944 we sensed that the Germans were beginning to toughen up, and it was all downhill from then on. On 22 January, some escape materials were discovered during a snap search in one block, and all of the occupants were evicted for two weeks, forced to double up in other crowded blocks.

On 8 February we got our first escapee out. Shorty Spires managed to hide in a wagonload of trash and survived the usual ramrod prodding by the ferrets as the cart went through the gates. Shorty had been equipped with money, a travel pass from a nearby work site, and a simple ID. He spoke good German and got to Vienna on a train from our local station. He ran out of luck in Vienna and could get no help, even at St. Stephen's Cathedral. Eventually, he was caught and returned to the cooler. The Germans would not believe that he was gone, so we had a bad time with tedious picture appels (each *kriegie* was matched against the Germans' photograph of him) until suddenly the authorities in Vienna called and told our commandant to send people to pick Shorty up and return him to camp.

During the winter of 1943–1944 we were working on a dreadfully dangerous escape plan that was the idea of, and would be led by, none other than Jerry Sage. He and four others, including Ed Tovrea and Buck Inghram, were to scale the south wire at night, departing from the block next to the theater with ladders, planks, and blankets to get over the wire. The scheme required lots of support. We needed to put the perimeter lights out and mount two simultaneous, spectacular diversions to fool the goons in the boxes on each side of the action, along with the "stroller" outside the wire between these boxes. These were formidable challenges,

Oberfeldwebel Hermann Glemnitz. This photo was taken through a louver in the attic of one of our blocks without Glemnitz's knowledge. I showed it to him at one of our reunions and he was astounded.

and I was very uneasy about the idea, but Jerry and his gang had practiced their drill endlessly and were gung ho to go.

We had studied the power lines connecting the lights, and, as they were bare wire, we had determined that to short them out all we had to do was pull them together with a grappling hook. The team assigned this job, headed by Lt. Col. Willy Aring, was ready. Davy Jones and I were left with the unavoidable duty of providing the diversions. Davy agreed to organize the east diversion with a fight, and I had to stage the west diversion. One of my men, a wonderful, enthusiastic guy who was game for anything, had agreed to be set on fire (suitably insulated) and jump screaming out of a west window of the theater at the carefully timed moment. Everything was ready to go when, after dark one night, half the perimeter lights suddenly went out. I couldn't believe it. This meant that there were

Christmas Greetings

Herr
"Arch Enemy"
but now
true friend
Hermann
Glemnitz

and
Best Wishes
for the New Year

A Christmas card I received from Hermann Glemnitz in about 1980. We had had a very friendly meeting at a previous reunion and I had sent him and his family a card as well. This is a copy of a caricature of Hermann done in the North Camp by Henry Picard, a gifted Belgian artist. Picard was lost in the tunnel escape of March 1944.

at least two circuits and that one grappling hook thrown over the wires could not darken the whole perimeter. I had the feeling that Glemnitz was giving us a message. When I went to Berlin in 1977 with Dick Schrupp, a second lieutenant shot down in the Mediterranean in March 1943 who spoke fluent German, to interview and prepare an oral history with Glemnitz, he said that he was not aware of our plan. At the time, however, I was very happy to abandon the idea.

By this time Sergeant Glemnitz had become an important person in my life, in that all of us were involved in escape activity. We knew him well and respected him. He was a good soldier and would have been one in any country's armed forces. He had been a pilot at the end of World War I, so he understood the restlessness of young airmen. He was never arrogant or bullheaded like so many of his underlings, but was shrewd and dedicated to his job of keeping us in. By the time we left Stalag Luft III in January of 1945, he and his ferrets had found about one hundred tunnels in our camps before they were completed. He only missed three, and one of those was the mass escape of March 1944.

☆ ☆ ☆

We completed the camp theater in mid-February 1944. It could seat 500 *kriegies*, and we were very proud of our work. It had heat, light, a projection booth, and an orchestra pit. The comfortable seats were made from the wooden boxes that the food parcels came in. I laid the bricks for the projection booth chimney, and I was very pleased when the chimney came through the precut hole in the roof as it was supposed to. I put my name and the date on the crown. The theater was a very important facility and performances were scheduled every night, including wonderful little theater productions, concerts, and the playing of records we received from home, which usually drew a full house.

In one small end-room in the theater we established a situation room. The walls were covered with maps of the various battle areas and interesting articles about the war. We were careful to keep the room free of any of our secret daily BBC communiqués, since the room was always crowded with *kriegies* and often Germans as well. The room was managed by Don Eldridge and Ed McMillan, and they put their heart into providing the camp with a first-class

South Camp theater. German photograph, courtesy of the Air Force Academy Library

A little theater cast. German photograph, courtesy of the Air Force Academy Library

facility. Don's postwar career was with Rand McNally, and he retired as one of its vice presidents.

We offered a broad program of professional education, and it became very popular. *Kriegies* with interesting experiences or special expertise gave talks or lectures to a full house on regular occasions. Davy Jones was asked to tell about his Tokyo raid. I knew his story well, since I had been his roommate for a while, so I set up, without his knowledge, a little extra pizzazz for his show. I secretly stationed all of the percussion instrument players under the stage with their drums and cymbals, and I positioned another man at the theater light switch. In a front seat I had placed a little man all made up like a Japanese soldier. I then introduced Davy and sat with him on the stage. It was a very proper affair with podium, glass of water for the speaker, and so on. I knew that when Davy told his story he always shouted "bombs away" at the climax, so all my troops were keyed to spring into action at that moment. Sure enough, when Davy spoke the magic words, all hell broke loose in the theater. The lights went out, and when they came back on, they illuminated a sea of frightened faces in the front row. The little "Jap" scurried up on the stage and confronted Davy with the question, "You Tokyo Jones?" Davy was a little shaken, but admitted that he was, and the little guy said, "Emperor Hirohito authorize me punch your ticket." It brought down the house.

Carolyn and I have been close friends with Davy and his wonderful wife, Nita, ever since the war, and we have been stationed together several times. But Davy never forgot my practical joke. Years later when we were both generals and I was making a presentation at Eglin Air Force Base where he was assigned, he arranged a similar interruption of my presentation to a theater full of officers. The lights went off, and a little guy dressed in a German uniform with a tin hat ran across the stage shouting epithets in German. Davy was not even in the theater at the time, but I found him at lunch and said, "Okay, now we're even." He agreed.

We had a lot of hilarity in camp and some fairly raw humor. I recall the day during a picture appel where we each had to be matched against our photograph. When Cy Widen's turn came he stepped smartly up to the table to be matched against his German ID card. He had two half ping-pong balls snapped into his eye sockets over his eyes. When the goon at the desk looked up, he almost had a heart attack. They took Cy off to the cooler.

From time to time, men received the inevitable "Dear John" letter from a girlfriend, advising that she had grown tired of waiting and had married someone else. Sometimes the recipient would post his letter on the bulletin board. One such letter appeared in which the young lady announced that she was sorry about it all but had married his father. She signed it, "Love, Mother"!

All of our American camps, I am sure, produced a newspaper at weekly or biweekly intervals. These were produced by men with journalistic talents and training. The papers were usually one or two large (1¹/₂ by 2¹/₂ foot) sheets of typed columns and color illustrations—some portraits, but most often cartoons. Although these newspapers were censored before publication, they were of great interest, and large crowds would form to read them as soon as they appeared on the bulletin boards. Regretfully, only about a one-year collection of the Center Camp's papers reached home and are now part of the U.S. Air Force Academy POW Historical Collection. They show in the best possible way the daily life, main interests, and humor of camp life.

There were many very gifted men in all of our camps. Small groups of well-educated men interested in cultural, philosophical, or political subjects formed discussion groups. Padre MacDonald, Dick Klocko, Bill Barnes, and Roy Dedman were generally recognized as possessing about the finest minds in camp, and their discussions were often over my head. Some *kriegies* were accomplished artists and eventually had their works published after the war. Others were clever with their hands and made the most remarkable things. One made a guitar, another a violin, and another constructed a steamboat that won a bet by successfully steaming around the fire pool. John Bennett brought with him his compass manufacturing operation from the North Camp. Potential escapees were equipped with these compasses, which even had "Made in Stalag Luft III" stamped on the bottom. Some men wrote beautiful poetry. One army GI who was captured at the Salerno Landing wrote excellent poetry and prose. He was in a different army camp, but some of his poetry was published in a *kriegie* newspaper distributed by the Germans. I saved several pieces of his work, and one poem that I especially liked follows:

It's not so far away
Four thousand miles, you say?
Why, it's just a heist and a belly crawl
To an upper bunk by the barracks wall,
At the dreamy end of day.

It's not very far
A sea spans where they are?
Why, I only have to let out sail
And hang my shoes on a rusty nail,
And follow the Western Star.

It was not so long ago,
An endless year or so?
Why just last night, I yawned and then
In thirty winks was home again.
I wonder, do they know?
—Frank Stebbing, POW, 2/3/43

Another *kriegie* wrote the following, and I regret that I have lost
his name:

The Lately Come

Peter was tired, his very halo drooped,
And so the Lord bent an attentive ear;
"It's all the flyers, Sire, I'm plumb wore out.
Couldn't we somehow get them out of here?
They zoom and shake the minarets of heaven
And think it's fine to break a serried rank
Of seraphim; they hedgehop in the golden streets.
I caught them teaching Michael how to bank!
The Ten Wise Virgins' lamps keep blowing out,
They stir up so much breeze; and who's to blame
For all that recent trouble with the Foolish Ones?

Indignant Peter blushed with honest shame.
And Zeus reports that his Elysian Fields
Are all cut up with the landings, and the asphodel
Is ruined for this season. Please you, Sire,
Can't Lucifer take over for a spell?"
The Lord looked thoughtful, watched the sunset sky,
Where unregenerate newcomers yet soared
In gay formation, giddy echelons,
While Old St. Peter murmured wildly, "Lord!"
And then he leaned down from his golden throne
And straightened Peter's halo with a smile,
"Peter, they were all very young, you know;
We'll let them play a while!"

—Author unknown

☆ ☆ ☆

Early on, we found that we needed to censor all of the outgoing mail. This was to ensure that information damaging to our war effort or to our clandestine activity in camp did not get passed to the German censors. A classic example of the naiveté of some of our young men was caught by our censors in the North Camp after the tunnel Tom was found by the Germans. Some lad had written to his mother saying, "Today the Germans found *one* of our tunnels!"

The German censoring of our mail was a serious intelligence operation under the supervision of the German staff intelligence officer and closely linked to the function at Dulag Luft, the German interrogation center. The Germans were interested in our letters from home, as they might contain information on troop movements, home morale, or shortages of critical materials. They were also interested in keeping their fingers on our pulse in camp, feeling that they might be able to gain an advance warning of a tunnel break or any suspicious group action. The censors were all women who had been English majors in college and had been drafted for the work. We never saw them, but we were sure that they were all beautiful young ladies. Each of them always handled the letters of the same *kriegies*, so they got to know us and our families. They used a stamp that appeared on all of the letters that passed through their hands. My censor was *Gepruft* (approved) number 43.

Only on one occasion during the entire time that I was a *kriegie* did we have an opportunity to glimpse one of these women as a real human being with feelings. The wife of one *kriegie* sent letters that were always filled with complaints and bad news—the kids were sick, the roof leaked, she couldn't pay the rent, and so on. One day one of these letters came in and down at the bottom next to the censor's stamp was a little note which read, "Dear Lieutenant, I have come to expect these letters. May God bring you home soon to this woman."

Some thirty-five years after the war we discovered that these ladies also had reunions, and we established a very warm relationship with them. We were invited to attend one of their reunions, and Dick Schrupp and I went. We had a great time, and later six of them attended one of our reunions. I have remained in touch with several of them ever since.

☆ ☆ ☆

In early March 1944, Moose Stillman rejoined us in South Camp. We had roomed together in the North Camp, but he had chosen to go with Del Spivey when the new American Center Camp opened in October 1943. After that, Moose managed somehow to be accepted as a volunteer to go to the American enlisted men's camp at Krems in Austria. He escaped in Bavaria en route, was recaptured after several days, then was brought back to Stalag Luft III and placed in South Camp. We had begun to suspect that South Camp was now regarded as the "bad boys' camp," as we noticed that we were seldom favored with privileges, such as beer at Christmastime, that were given to the other camps. Moose returned to be my roommate, and we were together until the end of the war.

Moose was very active in our escape activity, but his most visible and important contribution to the camp was the system of internal camp streets that he built. They literally lifted us out of the mud. He led a group of willing volunteers who raised the level of the interblock streets about eight inches above the surface of the local terrain, thus eliminating the chronic wet feet all of us had suffered from as we walked around the camp. This engineering feat was called "Stillman's *Strasse*."

☆　☆　☆

One day Glemnitz paid me a visit in my room and told me that in a surprise night bed check in one of our blocks the previous night he had found two men in one bed, and he wanted to know what I had to say about that. I simply shrugged it off. It would have been most unusual if, among 2,000 young men, even in the military, one found no homosexuals. While none had come to my attention, I was not surprised. I later discovered while serving as the director of military personnel for the Air Force that the homosexuals whom we were constantly processing out of the service tended to "nest up," so when we found one we usually found several more. Our adjutant, Mel McNickle, may have been aware of the situation since he handled room assignments and men were always changing rooms for one reason or another. To my knowledge we never had trouble over this issue. So if there was such activity, it was very discreet, something that was hard to achieve in our crowded camp.

A typical percentage of the *kriegies* in our camp were Jewish. This was noted on their dog tags so the Germans knew who they were. In the officers' camp, Stalag Luft I, the Jewish *kriegies* had been segregated. Because of strong protests from all of the other *kriegies*, however, they were not moved from the camp. There were enlisted Jewish POWs at other camps who were pulled out of the crowd and sent to work with Jewish slave labor, and some, I believe, were worked to death. To my knowledge, the issue never came up at Stalag Luft III.

☆　☆　☆

Sex and women were prime subjects of conversation only when food was abundant. When we were hungry, food was much more on everybody's mind. Pinup art flourished, but very seldom did I run across anything offensive. Some of it was very high class and some always appeared in the camp newspapers. Ribald discussions and arguments about sex always indicated that we were getting enough to eat.

We had serious fights from time to time, and we developed a standard method of handling them. The block commander would give each of the two combatants a pair of heavy boxing gloves and take them to the "ring," a place with deep sand that was reserved for such fights. The fights seldom lasted more than five rounds. Peer pressure, I think, helped to avoid any widespread bitterness or hatefulness in South Camp, at least.

☆ ☆ ☆

It was late afternoon on 24 March 1944 when I was called out to the north wire. Someone walking the circuit passed the word that Roger Bushell wanted to talk to me. I went out immediately, and Roger was standing there waiting. He called to me over the wire. "We go tonight," he said, then added, "Please don't do anything to screw it up." I assured him that our escape group had nothing planned and wished him good luck.

This breakout came to be known as the Great Escape. A number of good books have been written about it, but few, in my opinion, have given enough attention to the terrible risks and stresses that each individual who went down into that dank, dark tunnel had to face. Several were extremely claustrophobic, and, for all but a few, it was the first time that they had ever been thirty feet underground in a tunnel dug into soft sand. Perhaps the worst of it was the one-hundred-yard crawl to an exit hole in dark and snowy woods deep inside a hostile land.

Little did they know as they started out that disaster awaited most of them. The tunnel was not long enough, and, at the last minute, when the exit hole was opened, the first man out discovered that the tunnel did not reached the woods. Each man's departure from the tunnel was thus made slower and immensely more hazardous. Out in the open, men leaving the tunnel could easily be observed by the strolling guard outside the wire who walked end-lessly back and forth between the two nearest goon boxes. At the nearest point in his path the guard was no more than thirty or forty feet from the tunnel's exit. Fortunately, he was watching south into the camp through the wire, not out, but the exit of the tunnel was dangerously close to the midpoint of his beat. As it turned out, seventy-six men were able to clear the area, and two or three were caught aboveground at the exit. Some fifty or sixty men, still head to toe in the tunnel, had to crawl backwards all the way back into Block 104, fumbling and thrashing in total darkness. It was a mir-acle that a serious cave-in did not block this awkward and very dangerous process.

I was lying awake and heard the shot that signaled the goons' discovery of the tunnel. It was about 5:00 A.M., and I knew this was going to have far-reaching effects for us all. Soon after unlock I went out, and the ferrets were all inside the compound. I asked the one we called Blue Boy, "*Was ist los*?" He appeared to be very excited and replied to the effect that there had been a tunnel escape from the North Camp. He kept saying, "*Ich wusste, Ich wusste*"—I knew, I knew! Nothing much happened to us that day, as the turmoil was concentrated in the North Camp. The Brits spent most of the day being counted, ID'd, and recounted as they stood out in the cold.

That night two shots were fired into our block by a guard on the wire. The bullets passed through a room full of sleeping *krie-gies* and on into a second block without hitting a soul. God was surely with us that night. We continued to be harassed with snap appels and block searches. We found ourselves spending a lot of time on the sports field in the cold and rain. On one occasion we had expected a block search and brought many clandestine items out to appel in order to protect them from the search, but the Ger-mans fooled us. It turned out to be a personal search, and we lost a considerable amount of contraband. I had concealed a radio tube in my hat, and it was confiscated with great glee. Many *kriegies* dropped their contraband and buried it by scuffing it into the soil with their feet. The goons in the towers were watching us and called attention to this activity. The ferrets would then run to the spot and dig around. Often it was a fake, and soon all of the goons were angry. After the appel was over, the goons raked the field and collected quite a lot of our valuables.

It was clear that the German garrison had been badly shaken by the escape and the Gestapo was breathing down their necks. We soon learned that Colonel Von Lindeiner had been sacked, was presently under house arrest, and was to be court-martialed. The new commandant was a tough guy named Colonel Braune, and he and Rojo were soon exchanging unpleasant words. The ferrets were getting more aggressive, and we had several confrontations. On 28 March, however, we received a new *Lager* officer, a pleasant Austrian, Hauptmann Galothovics. We were very pleased with the change, as Hauptmann Fehmer, the former *Lager* officer, was a very unpleasant man. He went to Belaria.

On 6 April the goons summoned Rojo Goodrich out for a meeting with the new commandant. He painfully told Rojo that fifty of the British officers from among the seventy-six who had escaped through the tunnel on 24 March had been shot. He said that it was the result of their efforts to either resist arrest or attempt to re-escape after having been captured. The commandant limply admitted that none had been wounded. We were all shocked by this dreadful news, and although I knew that it was the work of Himmler's thugs, I seethed with rage toward all the Germans. The Luftwaffe was quite distressed by the shootings, but made it clear that their responsibility had ended at the perimeter wire. Feldwebel Von Gutenberg came in to see me personally in the South Camp and told me, with barely disguised shame, about the atrocity. Both the Swiss Protecting Power and the International Red Cross representatives paid us a very welcome visit during April. Our senior officers had much to talk to them about.

We now know that a few days after my chat with Roger Bushell, he was back in the hands of the Gestapo. Of the seventy-six men who got out of the tunnel and cleared the area before the tunnel was discovered by the strolling guard, seventy-three were eventually recaptured, including Roger. He was one of fifty who were executed by a shot to the back of the head. The prisoners were being transported in small groups, handcuffed, and they were shot as they relieved themselves by the side of the road. I had known and worked with all of them, and regarded them among the finest men I had ever known. They were not all English, but all were serving in the RAF. They would all have become leaders in their own countries after the war had they survived.

The goons came in and tacked up a bulletin, bordered in red, saying that because of the gangster tactics of the Allied special forces, escape was no longer a sport. It went on to state that due to the many restricted areas in wartime Germany into which an escapee would inevitably stumble and be shot, further escapes by POWs would be very dangerous and we better knock it off and stay in camp.

The Brits soon received word from the Air Ministry that British POWs were released from their duty to attempt escape. We Americans received no similar guidance to my knowledge, but the enthusiasm about escape cooled considerably in all of our camps as well. On 7 April, all of the Stalag Luft III camps held memorial service formations for the executed escapees. Their ashes were returned, and, in due course, the Brits built a beautiful monument in our small cemetery to hold the fifty urns. This stone sepulcher stood about five feet high by six feet wide and three feet deep. Three large sandstone panels were erected at the top, engraved with the names of the fifty officers. A large white metal RAF albatross adorned the face. This impressive monument, less the metal albatross which was vandalized, probably by the Russians, survives to this day and is carefully maintained by the Polish people of Sagan (now called Zagen). The ashes of the fifty, however, now rest in a military cemetery in Posen, Poland. Shortly after the shooting of the fifty British escapees was announced, the Brits in North Camp initiated an official report of the affair to be surreptitiously transmitted to the Air Ministry. This

To all Prisoners of War!

The escape from prison camps is no longer a sport!

Germany has always kept to the Hague Convention and only punished recaptured prisoners of war with minor disciplinary punishment.

Germany will still maintain these principles of international law.

But England has besides fighting at the front in an honest manner instituted an illegal warfare in non combat zones in the form of gangster commandos, terror bandits and sabotage troops even up to the frontiers of Germany.

They say in a captured secret and confidential English military pamphlet,

THE HANDBOOK
OF MODERN IRREGULAR
WARFARE:

". . . the days when we could practise the rules of sportsmanship are over. For the time being, every soldier must be a potential gangster and must be prepared to adopt their methods whenever necessary."

"The sphere of operations should always include the enemy's own country, any occupied territory, and in certain circumstances, such neutral countries as he is using as a source of supply."

England has with these instructions opened up a non military form of gangster war!

Germany is determined to safeguard her homeland, and especially her war industry and provisional centres for the fighting fronts. Therefore it has become necessary to create strictly forbidden zones, called death zones, in which all unauthorised trespassers will be immediately shot on sight.

Escaping prisoners of war, entering such death zones, will certainly lose their lives. They are therefore in constant danger of being mistaken for enemy agents or sabotage groups.

Urgent warning is given against making future escapes!

In plain English: Stay in the camp where you will be safe! Breaking out of it is now a damned dangerous act.

The chances of preserving your life are almost nil!

All police and military guards have been given the most strict orders to shoot on sight all suspected persons.

Escaping from prison camps has ceased to be a sport!

The bulletin that the Germans posted in all camps after the March 1944 escape. Courtesy of the Air Force Academy Library

was not an easy task, as its security had to be assured during preparation and transmittal. Bob Stark, a New Zealander and a very old *kriegie*, was one of the North Camp code men who was involved in this task. When Carolyn and I visited with him and his English wife in New Zealand many years later, he told me several interesting stories about this report. He said that one of the new group captains in camp was given the report to review and carelessly left it on the table in his room one day when he went out to appel. He almost had a heart attack when the block was subjected to a snap search during appel, but upon return to his room he found the report undisturbed.

An exchange of *grands blessés*, or seriously wounded men, was imminent, and among those to be repatriated from North Camp were Group Captain Massey (the old senior British officer), recently returned from the hospital, and the old senior Church of England chaplain whose name I don't remember. Massey was asked to carry the escape report home and deliver it to the Air Ministry, but he declined, as he felt the risk of a personal search

The monument built in our small cemetery by the North Camp British kriegies *to honor the fifty men who were shot after their recapture. German photograph, courtesy of the Air Force Academy Library*

was too high. The chaplain was then asked to carry it and was assured by John Casson (still a key man in the British code work) that he need not worry. John borrowed the chaplain's book of all the sermons that he had delivered in camp and which he was planning to carry home with him. John added four or five new sermons to his collection, encoding the report into them.

Everything went well until the returning officers reached Lisbon. At that time the chaplain, a New Zealander, was, to his surprise, directed to take a ship for home rather than to England. At the last possible moment, Group Captain Massey relented and took the chaplain's sermons home with him where they were safely delivered to the Air Ministry. In due course North Camp received, through the mail, an acknowledgment of receipt of the "moving religious messages."

One night in late April 1944, Phil the ferret caught Bill Hall, an early Eagle Squadron *kriegie*, distilling booze. This practice had by then been outlawed by mutual agreement of the commandant and the senior camp officers. However, Bill gave Phil a taste, and one taste led to another until Phil was crocked. He staggered off to one of the outside latrines and passed out. He failed to appear when he was supposed to leave the camp, and a vigorous search by all the ferrets located him and dragged him out through a crescendo of *kriegie* hoots and hollers. We assumed that he was sent to combat duty on the East Front, for we never saw him again. The theater was then closed as punishment for our naughtiness towards the ferrets.

☆ ☆ ☆

On 9 April, we had a midday air-raid warning. This was a very exciting development, as it meant that the U.S. daylight bombing was now reaching deep inside Germany. We were all required to stay inside and close the shutters during raids. Everyone was peeking out trying to get a glimpse of our aircraft, and one of the enlisted orderlies, Corporal Miles, was carelessly standing in the open doorway of the cookhouse. A guard on the wire shouted at him to get in, but he didn't obey. He was shot and instantly killed.

Miles was the second casualty in South Camp and was buried with full military honors. The American flag, firing squad, and band were provided by the Germans. Not long after this, Hitler ordered that military honors be omitted at future "Luft Gangster" funerals.

On the 11th there was another daylight air raid, and this time a beautiful formation of Flying Fortresses (B-17s) flew right over the camp at about 5,000 feet. What they were doing that low I never was able to discover, but it was a great thrill for all of us. The fact that the 8th Air Force could penetrate and strike targets this deep into Germany made us realize that our daylight bombing strategy was now working. Several of my British friends who had insisted that the Americans could not sustain our daylight bombing called to me over the wire to admit that they were now believers.

On 27 April 1944, the West Camp opened. It was totally American, and the SAO was Col. Dal Alkire, age forty-two and the most

Five ferrets assigned to South Camp. German photograph, courtesy of the Air Force Academy Library

senior of our full colonels. He had served twenty years in the Air Corps and was shot down on 31 January 1944 over Italy as a bomber group commander. A cadre of older *kriegies* with experience in all of the essential functional areas was sent over to help Alkire and the other new *kriegies* get squared away. Some of our most capable men went over, including Lt. Col. Willy Aring, Maj. Hal Houston, Navy Lt. John Dunn, Capt. John Bennett, and Lt. Tex Newton. This was the first camp at Sagan whose members were all new *kriegies*. None of them had had the benefit of entering a camp with an already operating staff. It was very difficult for them. They needed help getting sleeping arrangements set up, learning how to cook, keeping clean, and relating to the Germans without unnecessary trouble.

Alkire quickly selected his block commanders and staff and soon established the necessary discipline in the camp. Each of the camps at Stalag Luft III had a distinctly different character that largely reflected the personality and the policies of its leader. Before the war was over, the West Camp was destined to have a more difficult time as a group, but I believe that was more a question of bad luck than bad management. Lt. Col. Paul Burton wrote an interesting book about the West Camp called *Escape from Terror*, published by Looking Glass Graphics in 1995.

South Camp began to settle down a bit after the "Great Escape" and its ensuing tragedy, but we were all on pins and needles. We knew, and the Germans knew, that an invasion in the west must be imminent. The German newspapers were full of the *Festung Europa*, the imposing fortifications that the Germans had built along the coast all the way from Holland to the south of France. The German commander was General Rommel, the "Desert Fox," and the defenses looked very formidable—we saw them constantly in the German media.

Harold Decker faithfully recorded the nightly BBC communiqué, and he was the first to hear the declaration the underground all over Europe had been instructed to listen for. It consisted of a brief phrase such as "the daisies are blooming." It announced the launching of the invasion and the time for all of the underground forces in the occupied countries to launch their all-out efforts to disrupt the Germans. Decker received the signal in the early morning hours of 6 June 1944 and reported it to me. I immediately reported to Rojo.

We decided to withhold the announcement until the Germans publicized it, as we knew the camp would go wild and we didn't want to confirm to the Germans that we were in radio contact with our forces. At about 10:00 A.M., the German war communiqué made the announcement including, of course, the news that the enemy landings were being driven into the sea. As expected, all of the camps did go wild. We could see, through the wire, the excitement in the North and the West Camps, and we could hear it in the Center and East Camps. None of us would have guessed that we would still be in the bag for another eleven months.

We all listened to and read the daily news avidly. The tension was palpable as our American forces approached the crisis of the

Harold Decker (left) and Ed McMillan at Straubing Airport on their way home. They are standing near the tail of the FW-190 that landed with a female passenger. Photo taken with a clandestine camera

breakthrough at St. Lô. The Germans became more lenient, and we could see in their eyes that the end was getting near. I went on a parole walk with a small group about this time, and we had a beer (nonalchoholic) in a big barn with our German escorts.

One of them was Oberfeldwebel Eidmann, an obviously well-educated and decent man. I engaged him in a serious conversation about the situation in Normandy. He recognized the significance of the forthcoming battle of St. Lô and expressed confidence that we would be stopped. He grudgingly acknowledged that if we broke through, it meant we were on the Continent to stay, and that, he believed, portended the ultimate defeat of Germany. After St. Lô, I never could make eye contact with this man again.

On 14 June, the Germans confiscated almost 57,000 cigarettes from our blocks on orders of the security people, claiming that the packages contained a system of codes. This was nonsense, and most of the cigarettes were returned in late July without apologies. On the Fourth of July we had a full day of fun and games, as was traditional. Colonel Stevenson returned from the hospital that day. He had been there ever since 29 December when he was shot through both legs. He was welcomed at the gate by the band and by some of our prettier *kriegies* dressed as hula girls. They threw leis around his neck. That evening the whole camp marched to appel in the suntan uniforms that we had recently received through the Red Cross. We looked very spiffy, and it was good for morale.

On 20 July, the attempted assassination of Hitler was announced in a German radio broadcast. When Hauptmann Galothovics came in the next day for the morning appel, he returned all salutes with the Nazi salute. He reluctantly explained that, on Hitler's orders, since the attempt on his life had been made by members of the armed forces, the military salute would hence-forth be *verboten* and only the Nazi Party salute would be used in Germany. The tension among the Germans was very visible. I wondered how long Germany could hold together while enduring so much trauma.

Then came the strange case of Gen. Arthur W. Vanaman, who joined us on 29 July 1944, about seven weeks after D-Day. Vanaman had the distinction of being the only American general officer captured by the Germans during the war, and the way he earned this dubious honor is an astounding story. We learned after the war that he was the intelligence staff officer (A-1) for General Doolittle's 8th Air Force in England. As such, he had been briefed on the Ultra codes, the highly secret, successful decoding by the British of the German High Command's communiqués. Consequently, to prevent the possibility of capture by the enemy, Vanaman and all other persons knowledgeable of the Ultra codes were prohibited from flying in combat. In spite of this, he participated in a bombing mission as an observer. He understood that it was to be a "milk run." Instead, the mission was attacked in force. His aircraft was hit and set on fire. He and several others bailed out while the remaining crew members managed to put out the fire and return safely to base without him.

Brig. Gen. Arthur Vanaman. Drawing by an unknown artist in Center Camp

The timing of Vanaman's capture was providential from my point of view. Moose Stillman and I had been discussing for some time the growing gravity of our situation. We were the hated "Luft Gangsters" who had indiscriminately killed innocent civilians and destroyed Germany's cities. The Gestapo was itching to get its hands on us. The Russians were getting closer. The Germans were beginning to dig fortifications around our camp area, and there we sat—thousands of healthy combat-trained airmen. We represented a big investment for our government, and we felt that our predicament should at least cause some serious thought concerning ways to protect if not recover us. We figured that the least they could do was send a real leader who had some clout with the Germans.

When I heard that a U.S. Army Air Forces general and an RAF air commodore (the equivalent rank) had both been shot down and captured in the same week in early July, I said, "There they are!" I was so certain that they had been sent that I bet Moose a case of Scotch whiskey on it, to be delivered after the war. We learned after the war that the air commodore, who was named Islaw Chapman, had evaded capture in France for some days while the Air Ministry frantically tried to recover him. Eventually he was wounded and captured, and he spent most of the rest of the war hospitalized. We also learned after the war that Chapman had been privy to the Ultra codes, curiously enough, so his capture and the capture of Vanaman caused great concern in high circles of the British government.

But then I learned that General Vanaman had served as our air attaché in Berlin until we entered the war, spoke fluent German, and knew Goering. I was sure that he had been sent to provide some real leadership for us. However Moose said, "I know Vanaman, and they would never have sent him!"

Vanaman was in the hospital at Hoemark for some time and was then taken to Berlin where he met his old friends. Unbelievable as it sounds, he claims that he was never seriously interrogated. Vanaman was properly worried about divulging secrets, since he tended to talk in his sleep. He said he put tape over his mouth at night. The Germans wanted to send him to a VIP camp, but he insisted on being sent to the camp with all other American airmen. He arrived on 29 July and joined Del Spivey and the other senior officers in Center Camp.

He was officially designated the senior Allied officer, and he established a pattern of visits to the other camps where he was welcomed and expected to note the endless complaints. It was presumed that he would take them up with the commandant. I must say I saw few results, and I don't think we saw Vanaman in South Camp more than twice before we departed in late January 1945. It soon became clear that Vanaman had not been sent to provide us with a leader who had stature and clout with the Germans. Disappointed, I faced the prospect of paying Moose the case of Scotch as soon as we got home, which I did. I found him a case of Johnnie Walker Black.

During the summer and fall of 1944, we were endlessly harassed by the goons. They issued new arbitrary orders limiting the number of cigarettes authorized for each room, placed limits on the amount of Red Cross food we could keep in our rooms as an emergency reserve, and called endless special appels. Some were to inventory our goon-issue items: knife, fork, and spoon; bowl; cup; and the small towel that had been taken from and later returned to us. Some of these harassment efforts were actually for the purpose of identifying us. We were getting very crowded, and several tents erected in August were filled with new arrivals. However, they were taken down again just one month later, and we were all crowded in together with bunks made into triple-deckers. On 21 September we went on half parcels from the Red Cross due to the lack of resupply from Switzerland.

There was some good news. General Patton was charging across France, and there were huge tank battles in the east with steady Russian advances. Four or five more *grands blessés* departed for repatriation, and our mock radio station with a mike hooked into the internal camp public address system began operating. It was Station KRGY, and the operators were men skilled as radio announcers. They broadcast music and news, just like stateside, and it brightened things up a bit.

The surprise landing at Anzio, Italy, in January 1944 led to nothing due to the lack of an aggressive follow-through. A young pilot from my 31st Group's 307th Squadron, based at Anzio, came into camp, and I knew things must have been pretty rough there since he didn't even know his squadron commander's name. He was Maj. Al Gillam, and we heard an interesting story about him. According to the story, a British wing commander dropped in to see Gillam at Anzio, which was under constant shellfire from the hills east of the American position. While at lunch, the Brit's brand-new Spitfire IX was whisked away, hidden, and replaced by one of the squadron's old VBs, which had been totally destroyed through a direct hit by an artillery shell. When the Brit came down to the line to depart, he was given the bad news that his aircraft had been destroyed. He had to find another way to return to his unit, and Al Gillam now had a fine new Spit IX.

☆ ☆ ☆

On 15 August 1944, the American 7th Army landed in southern France, and eventually some of Col. Ben Davis's black pilots started coming into camp. The Germans were hoping that there would be trouble, but there was none. I especially remember one of these young men because he told us he'd been listening to Lord Haw Haw when he said that if any black airmen were captured they'd be castrated. This man had been shot down while strafing the beaches near Marseilles and was injured when he crash-landed. He said that when he regained consciousness he was being carried out of a German medical facility. The first thing he did was to check his family jewels. They were still there.

One day I noticed this *kriegie* lying on his back, clearly in pain but trying to watch a Luftwaffe flying demonstration over the camp. We always rubbernecked these demonstrations. I asked the guy what his problem was, and he said he had a very sore neck. We sent him out for treatment at the lazarette, and the next time I saw him he was in a snow-white cast from the top of his head to his waist. His neck had been broken in his crash landing.

For many years after the war I wondered what had become of this man. One day in about 1985, the academy archivist, Duane Reed, told me that a black gentleman had arrived at the academy on a tour with a visiting group of important city leaders. As the group was being briefed by the archivist in the Gimbel Room at the library, this man was noticed leafing enthusiastically through the Stalag Luft III scrapbook. Suddenly, he appeared to be having a heart attack and Duane rushed over to check on him. Duane talked to him and discovered that the reason he was so excited was that he'd just found a picture of himself in the book. It was the same man. He was in good health, and we sent him a copy of the photograph. He and other former black *kriegies* regularly attended our *kriegie* reunions.

☆ ☆ ☆

By August 1944, South Camp had six full colonels and about seven lieutenant colonels among our 2,000 *kriegies*. It was not possible to find meaningful jobs for some of the latecomers. Among the full colonels who arrived after midsummer of 1944 were Little Joe Miller and Jake Smart. Both had remarkable stories. Little Joe, who was one of the shortest men in camp, was a bomber group commander. He was shot down over France in March 1944 and was in the hands of the underground long enough to make it to the Spanish border where he and his guide were captured. His guide was summarily shot, and he was taken by the Gestapo to the infamous La Frènes prison in Paris where he lingered for months. He was trying to convince the Gestapo that despite his civilian clothes and lack of dog tags, he was not a saboteur. He finally remembered the name of a German around-the-world flyer whom he had helped rescue from the Philippine Sea many years before. As soon as he mentioned the man's name, the attitude of his jailers changed. They drove him in a big black car to Dulag Luft and delivered him to the commandant who, fortuitously, was the brother of the Luftwaffe officer (now a senior general) whom Joe had rescued.

Col. Jake Smart had been on General Arnold's staff and was present at the Casa Blanca, Quebec, and Washington Conferences during which President Roosevelt and Prime Minister Churchill planned the progress of the war. Later, against his better judgment, General Arnold gave in to Jake's persistent plea to be given command of a bomber group in combat. On 10 May 1944, on one of his early missions, Jake was shot down, injured, captured, taken to

Col. Jacob S. Smart (center). This photograph was taken after the war when Smart, then a lieutenant general, was participating in the change of command ceremony on Okinawa as Major General Clark (right) took over command of the 313th Air Division from Major General Stillman in July 1963. Courtesy of the Air Force Academy Archives

the Hoemark POW hospital near Dulag Luft, and interrogated. To Jake's chagrin, his interrogator showed him a photograph that had appeared in a recent *National Geographic* magazine showing Jake in a group picture with the president and the prime minister at Casa Blanca.

Jake's interrogation then became much more serious and was taken over by professionals, some of whom obviously had come down from Berlin. When Jake joined us in July 1944, he was a very subdued man and he maintained a very low profile in camp. None of us knew about his earlier prominence, and he didn't say anything about it. After the war, however, he told me that he'd made a very dangerous personal decision, in effect, to match wits with the Germans during his interrogation. Although he knew the entire strategic plan and even the date and place of the forth-coming invasion landings, he concentrated on convincing his interrogators of the inevitability of their ultimate defeat. He described in impressive detail the massive forces being put together to that end and apparently took all the wind out of their sails. Soon, some of them began confiding to him their disgust with Hitler and the course of his war. Meanwhile they had learned nothing of the strategy or tactics that they were supposed to obtain from Jake.

On 20 July 1944, the abortive effort to assassinate Hitler occurred and the dragnet to gather up and hang the perpetrators spread fear throughout the army. Jake arrived in camp about that time, and one of the more friendly Germans, whom Jake had subverted, sent him a note warning him that he was under suspicion of involvement in the assassination plot. This, I now know, is why Jake kept his head down that summer.

Paris was evacuated by the Germans in August 1944, and all of the godforsaken inmates of the La Frènes Gestapo prison were packed into "forty and eight" boxcars (forty men or eight horses) and sent to the Buchenwald Concentration Camp in Germany. Among these unfortunates were about 200 American and British airmen who had been shot down over France and had evaded capture. They had managed to reach the hands of members of the French underground who were seeking to assist them in escaping back to England. These marvelously courageous patriots actually got 2,000 Allied airmen off the Continent and back to England during the war.

In this case, however, plans went awry, and these airmen and a number of the accompanying underground personnel were captured by the Gestapo. The members of the French underground were summarily shot, and the airmen, most of whom were in civilian clothes and without dog tags, were sent to La Frènes and automatically accused of being spies and saboteurs. They were questioned endlessly, beaten up, and threatened with death. In August, when the Germans suddenly had to evacuate Paris, these men were packed off with all of the other political and criminal prisoners and taken to Buchenwald, the infamous concentration camp where so many perished.

The Allied airmen remained in Buchenwald for about two months during which time they were treated as wretchedly as all of the political prisoners, including being constantly threatened with execution. Somehow the Luftwaffe staff at Stalag Luft III discovered that they were there and had them removed and brought to Sagan where they put them in with us. These men arrived on 21 October 1944 in very poor condition, some in striped suits and all with shaved heads. They brought with them ghastly stories of the brutal treatment and exterminations then in progress at Buchenwald and the other concentration camps.

At that time, the existence of extermination camps was news to most of the world, and we documented their stories very thoroughly in hopes of being able to notify our government of this horror. I brought out a copy of our interview with these men, sewn into the lining of my leather jacket. When I arrived in Paris I delivered it to the Military Government Headquarters there. By that time, however, it was no longer news. General Eisenhower had recently flown all of the leading American journalists over to see these ghastly camps (by then all liberated) for themselves.

During the fall of 1944 a lot of tension had built up in the camp and the goons had become increasingly edgy. The war was going badly for them, but they knew they were in it until the bitter end. They were quite aware of the implications of unconditional surrender to the Allies, and they were now motivated more by fear than anything else. The Gestapo and SS were shooting and hanging anyone showing symptoms of disloyalty or faintheartedness.

The Russians crossed the Danube in early September 1944 and reached the Vistula River at Warsaw that same month. They then stood by and let the Germans destroy the brave anti-Communist underground forces who, under Polish Gen. Bor Komoroski, made a heroic effort to save the city from the Germans. This battle was witnessed by a British *kriegie* who was at large during an escape

A group of airmen who spent some time in the Buchenwald Concentration Camp before joining us at Stalag Luft III. Photo taken with a clandestine camera

attempt and was holed up in Warsaw. He was recaptured and brought the story back. It lessened our admiration for the Russians considerably.

With all these things happening, it was obvious that the war was approaching a crisis that would sooner or later involve us. The slow retreat of the German forces from the vast eastern areas, especially the Ukraine and Poland, where they were hated for their brutal treatment of civilians, was followed by terrible bloodshed. The Germans were liquidating all the inmates of some concentration camps and populations of small towns where their withdrawals had been opposed. Our camp senior officers were aware of this and were deeply disturbed that, in the event our German garrison departed and abandoned us to the advancing Russians, the SS or the Gestapo might, with Hitler's support, use the opportunity to get rid of the hated Luft Gangsters.

Accordingly, all of Stalag Luft III's camps were developing desperate and possibly hopeless plans to defend us against some such brutal yet possible action. In South Camp our SAO, Rojo Goodrich, in late September 1944, called in Lt. Col. Dick Klocko, briefed him on the situation, and gave him the task of developing a planned resistance involving all of us, en masse, regardless of how hopeless, against some retreating German civilian or military force. We felt that the Germans knew they probably had nothing to lose, and, armed with automatic weapons and artillery, might seek to destroy us. Dick listened quietly to Rojo, said, "Yes, Sir," smartly saluted, and proceeded to work, in secret at this point, with a small group. Among them was Maj. Jerry Sage, who was quietly teaching some eager young men the "silent death" tactics that he was using behind the German lines in North Africa before he was captured. Thank God nothing ever came of this before we were evacuated by our German garrison on 27 January 1945 for our trek to Bavaria.

I was disheartened by the slow progress of our armies toward the Rhine River. September turned into December, and it became clear that I was going to be in this damned camp through the winter. Disappointment turned into real dejection when, on 16 December, Hitler launched his surprise attack in the Ardennes. I recall how important the weather conditions were to the initial success of the German attack. From time to time during the winter, huge arctic high-pressure fronts would burst out of the north in central Europe and push the foul weather back into Holland and Belgium. Then there would be rain and fog for days, making air-to-ground support operations almost impossible. We also noticed in the first week of December a great deal of fighter training activity in our area, with large formations flying in the clear, cold air above us. I believe this was in preparation for the German offensive that was soon to be launched.

My morale was rock bottom in the face of these developments. One cold night I woke up to hear the *Hund Fuhrer* stomping his feet in the cold right outside our room. It was the closest I ever came to a feeling of despair. I remember saying to myself, "My God, when are we ever going to get out of this place?" I began to feel better when the German drive was halted at Bastogne. Still, ours was a rather quiet Christmas.

It had been a bad year for us with short rations, continual harassment, and shootings. The North Campers were understandably having an especially bad time. On New Year's Eve, Moose Stillman and I decided to go through the wire and visit our old friends in the North Camp. It was my foolhardy idea, and I talked Moose into coming along against his better judgment. We were not locked up in our blocks until after midnight on this occasion, so the goons would not be in the camp. We dressed completely in white in order to be camouflaged by the three inches of snow that had fallen. We wore white knitted wool caps, white sweat suits, and we pulled white socks over our boots.

We entered the wire at the midpoint on the north fence. I had a very good pair of wire-cutting pliers, so we had no trouble cutting our way through the wire and bending all of the cut ends out of our way. We then slowly rolled across the sports field, remaining motionless when the lights from the two goon boxes at the opposite ends of the north wire swept the snow-covered field. We stayed in line with our long axis toward the boxes and the lights. It was almost one hundred yards to the buildings, and we got pretty dizzy along the way. Our biggest concern was our visible breath in the cold air.

We had a nice but brief visit with our old British friends and returned the same way. Ed Bland, who was the SAO in North Camp, saw us off. Hitler was making what I believe was one of his last speeches to the German people at that time, and it was being piped loudly into all of the camps. It was one of his typical rousing speeches. He finished right at midnight, and all of the guards in the goon boxes fired their machine guns. Fortunately, they fired them into the air. Moose became nauseated from the endless rolling. We got back without a hitch but neglected to close our hole through the wire. The ferrets found it several days later. They must have been puzzled by the lack of tracks in the snow, but there were no repercussions.

By January the Russian winter offensive was moving steadily west and the Ruskies were getting closer and closer to us. We were

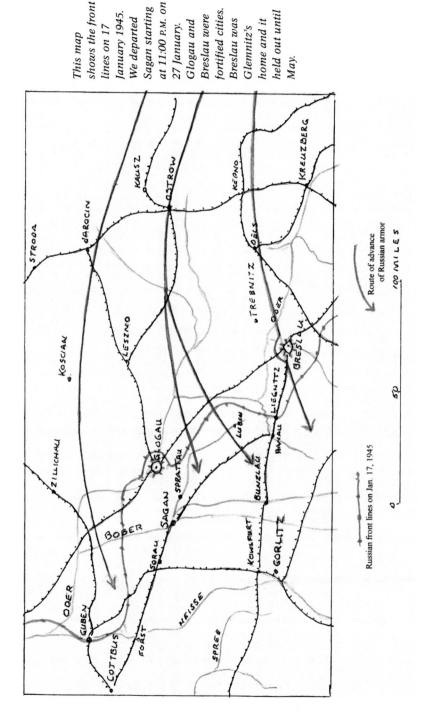

This map shows the front lines on 17 January 1945. We departed Sagan starting at 11:00 P.M. on 27 January. Glogau and Breslau were fortified cities. Breslau was Glemnitz's home and it held out until May.

Route of advance of Russian armor

100 MILES

50

0

Russian front lines on Jan. 17, 1945

all wondering whether the Germans would move us west or leave us to be liberated by the Russians. About mid-January, the Russians reached the Oder River, which runs northwest-southeast about fifty miles northeast of the camp, and we could hear the guns. We were all very excited, but our normal activities continued. The goons seemed stunned by the rapid advance of the Russians. Their behavior became more and more volatile.

We had directed everyone to prepare for marching. They were to have two pairs of long johns, two pairs of wool socks, a wool cap, a hood sewn onto their overcoats, a prepared pack, and a pair of shoes that were in good shape. The Red Cross had issued us all British airmen's kit bags, and we sewed shoulder straps onto them. Some men preferred to use a shoulder roll, in some cases making a pair of trousers into a shoulder roll. We all were urged to save chocolate bars and cigarettes for trading, to try to save some of our concentrated food items, and to walk the circuit to toughen up our feet. As the Russians got closer, it began to look like we might be left behind. We all felt extreme apprehension since we could not rule out some effort by the SS to liquidate us or take some other radical action.

I should mention here that in about November, Lt. Col. Willy Lanford had become the third resident of our little end room in Block 138. He'd been a bomber squadron commander and was in trouble because he'd continued a mission that had been recalled. His squadron went on alone and had serious losses including him, his aircraft, and his crew. He was in charge of the carpentry work in camp. A few days before we were ordered out, I expressed to him my regret at having to abandon my collection of clippings from the German papers and magazines. By then it amounted to two large scrapbooks and a large volume of about twelve issues of a Luftwaffe magazine that I had bound myself. This collection just filled the heavy cardboard Red Cross parcel box which, I believe, held four standard food parcels. Willy Lanford indignantly said that I couldn't abandon that stuff. I told him that I would give anyone who thought he could get it home for me a case of whiskey after the war. He grabbed the box and ran off with it to the carpenter's shop. When I saw it next, it was the first item tied on to his sled. That sled would become particularly important in the days ahead.

Then it happened. We now know that Hitler had previously given the order to move all of the Luft Gangsters west to prevent them from being liberated by the Russians. This had caused great hardship among the American and British enlisted airmen who had been held in large camps in East Prussia and Poland. Some had already been moved out and had been on the road for some time. Others had been crowded into ships at Baltic ports such as Danzig and moved west.

Now it was our turn. The German commandant's messengers brought the word in to all camp senior officers during the evening of Saturday, 27 January, at about 7:30 P.M. Rojo Goodrich shuffled onto the stage in the theater wearing his Dutch wooden shoes and interrupted a production of *You Can't Take It With You*. He simply said, "The goons have just told us that we are to leave in thirty minutes." This started a panic of preparations and stashing of food. My people had the additional task of recovering our vital clandestine stuff from various hiding places and arranging for as much of it as possible to be taken with us. Our money; radios; batteries; cameras and film; tools such as wire cutters, hacksaws, tin snips, and prangers (makeshift hammers); maps; master travel and ID papers; and so on all had to be packed up. Everything was in the hands of designated carriers or in known hiding places, which included tin cans buried in the frozen ground. Davy Jones had money in those cans, and he built fires over them so he could thaw the soil and dig them out. Ferrets then came and warmed their hands over the fires, seriously delaying the job. Fortunately we did not actually leave the camp until 11:00 P.M.

The same hectic action was taking place in all the camps. Everyone was ripping apart their homemade comforters to separate the good GI blankets from the shoddy German ones. They hurriedly packed their kits, ate the food they couldn't take with them, and stoked everything flammable into the stoves. We had been cold for a long time and knew that we would soon be much colder. Everyone huddled around the stoves trying to get as warm as possible before facing the bitter cold ahead. After lining up at the gate, we stood stomping and shivering for a long time before we were marched out. Ours was the first camp to move out, and then, at intervals, the others moved out until the last one, East Camp, departed at about 6:00 A.M. We have since learned that the Belaria Camp, which was the last camp to be activated and was located some distance northwest of Sagan, did not leave until that evening.

CHAPTER 9

The Trek to Bavaria

27 January to 5 February 1945

I won't ever forget the exhilaration I felt as we trudged out the gate. I didn't care where we were going; I was just so glad to be leaving that wretched camp. Several inches of hard-packed snow covered the ground, and more snow had begun to fall. As we walked past the North Camp we saw that Block 104, from which the tunnel Harry had been dug, was burning furiously. No one made any effort to control the flames, and the rows of blackened chimneys stood out starkly in the night. I feel sure that the Brits had burned the block deliberately.

We marched west on the little road that marked the north boundary of the camps and passed the cemetery and the Russian camp, but I couldn't see any activity there. We turned southwest on a narrow road and soon halted. The goons issued some bread and other items from the camp kitchen. The loaves of bread weighed about three pounds each. The men quickly cut them up and shared the hunks. A horse-drawn wagon followed the column. By this time Rojo, Mel McNickle, Lou Parker, Moose Stillman, and I, at Willie Lanford's invitation, had placed our packs on his sled. That made the load about waist high. It appeared to be stable, but it would require two men pulling and two pushing for the next four days. That was still much easier than carrying the packs on our backs.

Rojo had decided to stay with his staff at the tail end of the column since he felt that if there was trouble, the rear was where it would occur. During the pause, Rojo and I found a discarded five-pound block of German ersatz honey. Nobody wanted to carry that

South Camp kriegies *on the march, 28 January 1945. This photograph was probably taken by John Bennett or Dick Schrupp with one of our clandestine cameras.*

block, and it was too hard and messy to try to cut it up into smaller portions, so we squatted down on our haunches right there in the road and ate as much as we could. The honey was cold and quite solid, so we just gnawed away at it. Nearby, two *Hund Fuhrers* had allowed their dogs to get too close together, and the two huge Alsatians were engaged in a fierce fight with their jaws locked. What an improbable scene this would have presented to a neutral observer had there been one in war-torn Germany in the middle of that cold and snowy night in January 1945.

Soon we all stood up with the goons shouting, *"Raus mit"* and started moving forward. We had no idea where we were bound or how long we would be on the road. Within an hour or two, debris began to appear along the sides of the road. Items were slowly discarded by *kriegies* who decided they must lighten their loads of cherished possessions, things they'd hoped to take home. Musical instruments, beautiful models of boats and airplanes, books, and even food and clothing were strewn along in the dirt. I was among those who decided to lighten the load, and I made one of my most difficult decisions of the war. Along with several other items, I took out Carolyn's wonderful letters that were all wrapped in a waterproof packet. I kissed them first and then threw them over my shoulder. After the war, reading my own dull, sterile letters, I came to realize that I had discarded an irreplaceable treasure. Inspiring and loving, those letters reflected the great courage and devotion of my dear wife. She never mentioned her problems, the illnesses of the kids, or her difficulties trying to survive on a totally inadequate allotment.

Every hour or two we paused for a few minutes. The column had begun to settle down, but the pace was too fast and there was a lot of tiresome backing and filling. Soon some men were lagging and complaining, and suddenly a man was down, being stepped over as the tail end of the column approached. Everyone kept urging him to get up as they passed, and when he saw the end of the column he got up. He probably ended up in the horse-drawn wagon following our column, but we were very uncertain about how the goons would handle stragglers. Some thought they might be shot. That man who fell out was one of the few who did not prepare properly for the march. He simply tossed all of his stuff in a mattress cover and threw it over his shoulder. I remember another *kriegie* complaining to Lou Parker, fearful that he wasn't going to make it because he suffered from severe hemorrhoids. Lou suggested that he just tuck them back up inside and carry on, which he did.

After the first few hours, Rojo moved our small group of senior officers to the head of the column in order to slow the pace. We found Unter Officer Hoendahl leading the column with a tommy gun slung across his chest. Only about thirty-five, he had grown up as a Hitler *Jugend* and had been on the camp staff from the early days, giving us nothing but trouble. I don't recall there being another German officer with our column, and I suspect that Hoendahl enjoyed a special status.

We walked until about midmorning. It became apparent that the goons had made no plans for the march, since there were no arrangements to stop where we could find shelter and hot water.

Edward D. "Bo" Shaw during the march from Sagan. Photograph taken with one of our clandestine cameras. All the photos taken on the march involved considerable risk, as the goon guards were walking along beside us.

The orders from Berlin had obviously caught the Germans unprepared.

Finally we came to an enclave with several large barns, and the farm folk were kind enough to provide us enough hot water for cups of our Red Cross Nescafé. We ate some goon bread with canned meat and munched on D-bars, nutritious chocolate ration bars reinforced with oatmeal. These were contained in all Red Cross food parcels. This was the way we continued to eat for the rest of the trek. Moose and I curled up in a pile of straw on the floor of a barn and tried to sleep, but it was very cold. We did manage to get a little rest before we were off again shortly after noon.

I believe we walked until about dark and then stopped at another farm cluster where we obtained hot water. After eating some of our rations, we bedded down wherever we could. Some of the men made deals with the locals and traded cigarettes and chocolate for eggs and hot soup. I slept in a chicken coop with Rojo and one of our enlisted men. We had to crawl in, and we were very crowded. I remember that the GI mumbled and moaned all night long in his sleep.

From the very start of our march, we found ourselves accompanied by hundreds of refugees all heading west to avoid falling into the hands of the Russians. The German "pioneers," whom Hitler had sent east to take over the farms of the unfortunate Poles, many of whom were now slave laborers all over Germany, were all terrified of the Russians. With wagons drawn by scrawny, exhausted horses, they filled the roads and were a pathetic sight, much worse off than we were. Many had obviously been on the road for a long time and were as exhausted as their horses. At one stop where we were in a crowd of these miserable people, I watched a *kriegie* take off his wool gloves and hand them to a weeping little girl who walked behind a wagon holding her bare, frostbitten hands. In this same crowd I saw a strange and incongruous sight: a lovely young woman, wearing a fur coat and hat, riding alone in a wicker pony cart drawn by a well-fed little horse. She was very impatient to be on her way, but we were all being held up by a passing military convoy. I still wonder who she was and whether she ever made it to safety.

The interruptions along the road were constant, and with a cry of *"Von links heran"* (give way to the left), we all hit the ditch when military vehicles passed. Most of them were also heading west. We were being pushed hard by the goons, as all of the other columns were following us, and the five camps must have stretched out for twenty miles. There was a possibility that the Russians might overtake us. In violation of the Geneva Conventions, which specified that POWs were not to be marched more than twelve and a half miles in twenty-four hours, we marched thirty-five miles in twenty-seven hours.

Del Spivey's Center Camp got a late start the following day and spent the night in the small town of Halbau. The townsfolk kindly opened up their small church as the only available shelter. Most of the 2,000 *kriegies* stuffed themselves into this small church, and others spent the night outside without shelter. General Vanaman slept on the alter. Years later Colonel Spivey, who had since become a major general, returned to Halbau, now Polish and Catholic, with a small group of his former *kriegies* and presented the town with a stained glass window for the little church.

Several times I suggested to Willie Lanford that we should chuck the big box of my scrapbooks off his sled, but he adamantly refused. It must have weighed twenty pounds. I remember one stop on a road covered with glazed ice and snow when Rojo lay down in the road groaning with pain from his back, which had been broken when he bailed out of the top hatch of his bomber. He hadn't been without pain since. None of us really knew how cold it was, and many later exaggerated it. But it was cold enough to form frost around the edges of our hoods. I would guess it went down well below freezing at night.

The first night we walked and the second night we rested. On the third night we walked again and were getting very tired and cold. As we trudged along sometime after midnight, a *kriegie* suddenly trotted past us without a word and continued up the road. Hoen-dahl started to unlimber his tommy gun and I ran after the *kriegie* and tackled him. We fell by the side of the road as the column continued. I got the lad on his feet near the middle of the passing column but he wasn't rational. We must have been passed by his group, for some were calling to him. I took his pack and we joined the column. I stayed with him until we reached another pause. He seemed okay, so I gave him back his pack and returned to the head of the column. I never knew who he was until one day about forty-three years later he visited the Stalag Luft III POW Historical Collection at the Air Force Academy Library. I happened to be there that day and, with a film of tears in his eyes, he reminded me of the incident.

The pause had come just as we were entering the town of Muskau. We stood in the cold for almost two hours while the goons searched for shelter. The obvious solution was a large factory that made ceramics, glass, and earthenware. Most of the employees were French and Polish. There were numerous buildings in this facility, all offering some shelter and warmth. The blast furnace was burning, and once the manager opened the gate we staggered into the compound and entered a number of the buildings. Many men collapsed without even taking off their packs. The wait in the cold had produced some frostbite, and we were in urgent need of rest.

Our small group entered a round, glassed building that turned out to contain the central furnace for all of the high-temperature work at the plant. It was very hot in there, but we didn't care. As exhausted as we were, someone had to see that all the men got into a building with some heat. I remember that Col. C. D. Jones got up on a high spot and tried to establish some sort of order among the mass of *kriegies* who were crowding around the huge central furnace. Some were getting so overheated that they were passing out.

I went out and started checking around to make sure everyone had shelter somewhere. I remember finding Captain Williamson, one of our better block commanders, with his people in a coal storage room underneath the furnace. He had the entrance door open, as the air was poor in the room where his people were lying like cordwood. We decided that it was not carbon monoxide that we smelled, but he promised to keep the door open since the room was quite warm. Thank God, the next morning they were all okay.

I also checked on another big, high-ceilinged room where people were still staggering in. Near the door, large glass containers for storage batteries were stacked to the ceiling way above our heads. I watched "Doc" Heston Daniels, who had been an alternate pilot on the Doolittle raid, stagger against this mountain of glass. He almost brought it crashing down on our heads. After the war I learned that some of our people were taken in by the townfolk and did not reappear until we departed two days later. Among them was a West Point graduate full colonel whose help we could have used in making sure that everyone got in out of the cold. That night and the long wait in the cold after our arrival at Muskau were our darkest hours.

Rojo and I finally bedded down on the concrete floor of a large area full of machines used for shaping earthenware taps and spigots. The next morning we moved with the sled to another building where there was a modern washroom with hot water. We all cleaned up and shaved, and that night we slept warm for the first time since leaving Sagan. I first realized how exhausted I was while helping to carry our sled up a flight of stairs with Moose and several others. I suddenly had a palpitation of my heart. I sat down and it quickly went away. I haven't ever experienced this condition since, but it really worried me at the time.

I was confident then that we had not yet lost a soul on this forced march. Though that was true, I did learn later that Charlie Cook, one of our Eagle Squadron pilots, had cut his left hand and was very ill at Muskau with blood poisoning in his arm. He was only semiconscious when his buddies put him on a sled and dragged him to a hospital in town. He was refused admittance, and eventually was returned to Sagan by the goons in a lorry. There, he joined hundreds of other ill or crippled *kriegies* who could not march. Several British POW doctors had remained behind to care for these men, and Charlie's life was saved by one of them. He gave Charlie the last of his sulfa drugs and remained behind with several others who were too ill to be moved. Approximately 500 POWs who could be safely moved departed on 6 February. They were taken to Stalag XIIID in the suburbs of Nuremberg, where the West Campers had recently arrived. Charlie and the others who were left behind ended up being liberated by the Russians, who gave them proper care. When these men were strong enough, they were sent to Odessa and shipped home. Charlie told me this fascinating story after the war.

After the war I also learned, from reading Paul Burton's excellent book about the West Camp, *Escape from Terror*, that about fifty South Campers remained behind at Muskau when we left, and they joined up with West Camp. They probably had frostbitten feet, but I do not believe their feet were seriously damaged. All in all, I was proud of the performance of our camp on the march so far. What amazed me the most was the way the nonathletic types performed. They seemed to handle the march just as well as the jocks.

Somehow all of the camps were processed through Muskau, and the British *kriegies* were split off and sent north to the vicinity of Darmstadt and Luckenwalde. Since the war, I have learned that other facilities in and around Muskau were opened to the columns that followed South Camp. Chaos was everywhere, but there were many stories of kind offers of food and shelter by the townsfolk.

The goons were not much in evidence while we were in Muskau. I presume they were so pleased that they had not had a mass escape or some other hostile act that they felt very relieved. Additionally, they were preoccupied with their own problems, which were formidable. Some of their exhausted old soldiers had thrown away their rifles during the march, and in some cases *kriegies* carried their rifles for them. We don't know if any of these soldiers were lost during the march, but some were so old and feeble they could well have died.

South Camp moved out after two nights of rest and headed for Spremberg, about fifteen miles to the west. By this time the weather had warmed up and we were dragging our sleds over mud and cobblestones as well as snow and slush, but the walk to Spremberg was not hurried, and we all felt better after our rest. In every little town along the way we saw boys (Hitler *Jugend*) and old men (*Volks Strum*) training under arms to save Germany from the Russians.

At noon we entered an army compound set up for tank training. The tanks all had wood burners to provide gas for the motors. We were given wonderfully nourishing bowls of hot soup and then were assembled in a large area surrounded by barracks and vehicle sheds. While we were standing there, a messenger from the pottery plant arrived with an urgent request for the return of some leather belts that we had "liberated" from the machines. Our men were using them to pull sleds. Rojo called his block commanders front and center, and when they arrived they all gave Rojo their smartest hand salute. I noticed that the German officers who were around us winced visibly. Since the assassination attempt on Hitler, the Germans no longer allowed the military salute, so using the hand salute had added meaning for many of us. The belts were returned forthwith.

We arrived at Spremberg in the late afternoon of about 2 February, and it became clear that we were going to entrain the long line of boxcars next to where we had stopped. They were the usual forty and eights, but we were being forced to pack sixty or more men in each car, as there were 2,000 of us and only about twenty-eight or thirty cars. Most of them had recently carried cattle and had not been swept out, so our outlook was miserable. We had no brooms, so we had to settle into the mess. All the cars were so crowded that we could not all sit down, much less lie down. We had no idea where we were going or how long we would have to put up with the situation. It was a grim outlook indeed.

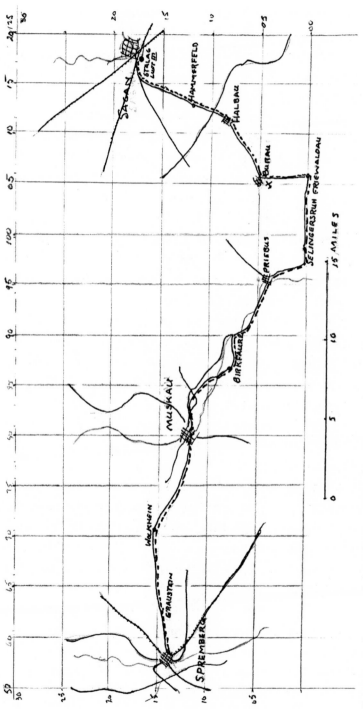

Route map of our march from Sagan to Spremberg. Drawing by A. P. Clark

Rojo and our small group of senior officers did not enter the lead car but instead found a car in the middle of the train that was relatively clean. We boarded the car and loaded the sled with all our food, packs, and the cursed box of my scrapbooks. I found a spot in the back corner of the car under one of the small windows that were located high in the opposite ends of each car and spent most of the time on my feet trying to see where we were going. The goons occupied the front and rear cars and posted sentinels on top of these cars. Following an orderly loading operation with little shouting and shoving, we were soon underway.

After the war we learned that when the Center Camp reached Spremberg a day or two later, General Vanaman, Colonel Spivey, and three other officers were pulled out of the column and told that they were going to be taken first to Berlin and then sent home via Switzerland as a reward for their peaceful and orderly conduct during the march. We also later learned that shortly after the arrival of Colonel Alkire's West Campers at Nuremberg on 5 February, the Germans asked for the names of five more *kriegies* to be sent home as a reward for the orderly performance of the camp on its movement from Sagan. Colonel Alkire picked the five oldest prisoners among his men, and they turned out to be my old friends from East Camp who were all shot down in 1942: Tex Newton, Pug Wheeler, Hub Croteau, Bill Frost, and Hal Houston.

Vanaman and this small group were taken to Berlin and, with grave misgivings and uncertainty, were left to cool their heels for weeks in the huge POW camp at Luckenwalde. Del Spivey tells the whole story in his fine book, *POW Odyssey*. Suffice it to say that eventually Vanaman and Spivey were wined, dined, and briefed by German generals and civilian dignitaries, all of whom were acting without the knowledge or approval of Hitler. They included some of Himmler's underlings along with General Berger, the SS commander of all POWs in Germany. Their pitch was that the United States and Great Britain should change sides in the war and help Germany save Europe from the barbarians approaching from the east. Vanaman and Spivey were then driven to Switzerland and put across the border on 23 April with messages making these proposals to be delivered to the Allied authorities. The other three officers, including Col. Bill Kennedy, Captain George, and Lieutenant Brown, along with the five who went to Berlin from Nuremberg, were all unceremoniously returned to join us in Stammlager VIIA at Moosburg.

General Gotlieb Berger, Waffen SS, in charge of all Kriegesgefangen *(POWs) in Germany. German photograph, courtesy of the Air Force Academy Library*

I have some vivid memories of the train trip from Spremberg, which lasted about two days and three nights. I remember passing slowly through Dresden. This was on about the 3 or 4 February. The city was a center of German history and housed a collection of priceless and irreplaceable art. I recall the old women dressed completely in black who were greasing the railroad track switches in the marshaling yards with a stick and a bucket of black grease. The city was filled with military hospitals and refugees from the east and was regarded as an open city. On 13 and 14 February, ten days after I passed through, Dresden was utterly destroyed by British and American bombers with great loss of life. Unfortunately it had become an important rail junction behind the advancing Russian lines, and Churchill decided that Allied support of the Russians was more important than the inevitable human tragedy. This was one of the few occasions when the American bombers departed from their normal strategy of hitting exclusively military targets and joined the RAF in destroying a city.

Sometime during the second day our train stopped on a curved track on an isolated siding and we were all let out to relieve ourselves. It was quite a sight—2,000 men all squatting in the snow with their pants down. Rojo chose this pause to move his staff to the head car. It turned out to be a dreadful mistake. We all traipsed through the field of feces carrying our sled on our shoulders and were filthy by the time we reached the new car. It turned out to be full of manure, so we were all a real mess. Rojo then had to go relieve himself again, and when he climbed out of the car he cut his hand badly and didn't discover it until he had his pants down. When he got back to the car he was in shock. We got him in and moved off with a lurch. Someone in the car had some medical dressings, so we fixed him up. But poor Rojo was never in very good shape again. He wasn't able to do much as our senior American officer from then on.

Sometime during the next day, we pulled into the station in Regensberg. In spite of our warnings, many men drank out of the big tubs holding water for the locomotives. Fortunately none of them became ill, but the water was dangerously contaminated and I was concerned. By then we knew that we were going to the Munich area. We were then only about 140 miles from Switzerland, so that night would be our best chance to escape. With Rojo's approval, I went down the line of cars while we were given a break and passed the word that anyone who wished to jump train was free to do so. Money, maps, and compasses were distributed.

While we were in the station, a German armored division that had been going the other way stopped on the next track. The men were traveling on the flatbed cars with their tanks. We figured they were on their way from the Italian front to the war in the west. These soldiers looked tough, and when they realized we were Luft Gangsters they swung the weapons on their tanks around and aimed them at us. If they had in fact just come through the Brenner Pass from Italy, they probably had good reason to be mad at us. The rail lines through the Brenner Pass had been subjected to continuous heavy bombing, as all of the *kriegies* who had come up as prisoners from Italy could testify. Fortunately the air-raid sirens started wailing and both trains hurriedly departed the station in opposite directions. One of the favorite Allied bombing targets was the fighter aircraft assembly plant in Regensberg, and it was probably about to get hit again.

That night thirty-two men jumped off the train and were apparently not detected—the train never stopped and we heard no shots fired. It took a lot of guts to make this escape considering our wretched physical condition and the uncertainties of a jump from a moving train into the night. We later accounted for all thirty-two men; every one was eventually caught and returned to camp. Several reached the Swiss border before they were apprehended. They all reported that it was extremely dangerous out there since our fighters were shooting up everything that moved along the roads.

CHAPTER 10

Stammlager VIIA, Moosburg

5 February to about 12 May 1945

ometime before dawn we pulled into a siding. After daylight
arrived we detrained and were marched about a mile through a
field, still carrying our sled like a litter with our packs and the box
of my scrapbooks stacked on top. We arrived at the main gate of
the big, old POW camp designated Stammlager VIIA. It was about
a mile northwest of the small town of Moosburg and about thirty
miles north of Munich.

Indifferent German army soldiers immediately searched us.
While we lost a few things, we found that a few American cigarettes
worked like magic in getting our stuff through the line. Most of our
logbooks were taken to be examined by the censors. When mine
was returned, some ten pages in which I had tried to give the history of other known POW camps had been cut out, and I was very
distressed. If I had been more skilled or brazen in the use of my cigarettes, I probably could have saved the book, but I was not very
good at bribery. Willie Lanford got the scrapbooks through without
any trouble, and the big box went under his bunk and stayed there
for the rest of the war.

We were then separated from all our clothing and gear and
herded naked into a big room with overhead shower outlets where
we took brief, warm showers. We were all shocked to see how
much weight we'd lost. I scrubbed Davy Jones's back and all his
ribs were showing. While we were in the shower all of our possessions were fumigated, but this was a useless precaution as we soon
discovered that the camp was heavily infested with fleas, lice, and

Aerial photograph of Stammlager VIIA taken by Allied reconnaissance aircraft.
Courtesy of the Air Force Academy Library

bedbugs. It was impossible to keep from being bitten by each in turn. That shower was the last proper one we would enjoy until the end of the war.

Stammlager VIIA was cut up into many *Lagers* separated from one another by barbed wire and locked gates. This arrangement was designed to keep men of different nations or ranks separated. None of the *Lagers* held more than about 1,000 men, so we were broken up into groups scattered among several *Lagers*, making control and communication initially very difficult. I ended up in a room with four double bunks occupied by Rojo Goodrich, Moose Stillman, Mel McNickle, Lou Parker, Joe Miller, and, I believe, Jake Smart, among others. About all we did for a while was rest and eat as much as we could get. That wasn't much, as the camp was on half rations. Stammlager VIIA held about 30,000 men at this time, and more were coming in daily.

Trading over the wire from compound to compound became a major pastime. We found that some of the old *kriegies* were working in areas that gave them special access to the people beyond the wire who were able to offer the things we really wanted, mainly food. Our cigarettes, chocolate, and soap gave us real buying power. Our senior officers made an effort to control inflation, but the old traders in the *kriegie* community knew all the tricks, and we usually got taken. Everything had to be negotiated between one of our people and a Russian, Serb, or Italian on the other side of the wire, and then the items were exchanged by throwing them over. Barter became a big business that attracted the skilled traders, and we let them represent us in most instances. I wanted a clean sheet and a good pair of scissors with which I could cut tin. I got them very promptly for a reasonable number of cigarettes in a transaction handled by one of our traders.

The German rations were the worst we had experienced, and we were on half the normal Red Cross food parcels. These parcels came out of a huge warehouse near town managed by old British and French prisoners under German supervision. We never had enough to eat, and I was hungrier than I had ever been. This was the first time we had been without enough food for any length of time, and the hunger caused us to do things we would never have done under normal circumstances.

I recall that Davy Jones traded his watch over the wire for a large package of oatmeal, a can of Klim (very rich powdered milk), and several D-bars. He cooked this all up and filled his big goon-issue bowl. I found him sitting up on top of a locker with his big tin spoon, happily eating away. I did something I was later ashamed of, demanding that he give me a spoonful, which he did. One man was caught stealing potatoes from the box of hoarded food belonging to his bunkmate. We told him that it was being made a matter of record and that he could expect to face a court-martial after the war. In retrospect, it is hard to comprehend the significance of such an act. Nothing came of it, of course, but I remembered who he was and could find no warm feelings toward him when he showed up at the reunions.

Poor Rojo had pretty much taken to his bunk. He wore his field jacket and a blue stocking cap, and he never took them off. He had little to say and usually got up in the night to nibble on his Red Cross cheese and D-bars. We worried about him, as he was no longer interested in what was going on. He probably rationalized that this was a big camp with a British and an American senior officer, both of whom outranked him, so he might as well relax.

Most of our men were utterly miserable. They were hungry, cold, discouraged, crowded, and being eaten up by the bugs in our dirty blocks. I remember talking to Nick Stoffel through the wire one day, and he complained about the bugs, then opened up his shirt so I could see the mass of fleabites on his chest. Nick was one of my most devoted workers, forging travel documents under very difficult circumstances. He said that all of the men in his filthy block were similarly bitten.

Soon, men were coming in who had been captured in Normandy shortly after the breakthrough at St. Lô. I ran into an army ground forces major whom I had known at West Point. He had

A view of our filthy, wretched camp. Courtesy of the Air Force Academy Library

been captured with his entire staff a few days after the battle. He sadly recounted how the assault had been preceded by a mammoth bombardment that had been off target and decimated his battalion in the front lines. On this occasion, U.S. bombs also killed the U.S. Army commander, Lt. Gen. Leslie McNair, who had been an observer in this major's sector. He told me how his unit, which was full of raw replacements, went on, but the men were so emotionally and physically exhausted that they had not fought well. They had been surrounded and captured only a few days after the battle.

I also met an impressive captain of the famous British 1st Airborne Division, which had parachuted into Arnhem in Holland in September 1944 and had subsequently been trapped. That division's survival depended on Allied forces taking one bridge too far, which didn't happen, and they were destroyed. He had recently arrived from the hospital, having recovered from serious wounds including the loss of his testicles.

We learned that Hitler had directed that Allied prisoners from all over be gathered in Bavaria. Hitler apparently had chosen the

Alpine area (the so-called Alpine Redoubt) to make his last stand, and he planned to hold thousands of Allied prisoners as hostages, including the diplomats, generals, and other important persons who were termed *Prominenten*, along with the Luft Gangsters. The camp was rife with rumors about the fortifications and weapons going into the redoubt, and some of it was true. We also heard the rumors that Hitler was planning to liquidate us. Sometime in early April all airmen prisoners were ordered to be ready to depart for the redoubt in two days. Our senior officers had decided, after painful debate, that we should not resist, as it might set off a slaughter in the camp. We were to start the trip moving as slowly as possible and hope that the end of the war would overtake us en route.

We began packing our kits and many attempted to fashion carts, having learned that pulling a cart or sled was easier than carrying a pack. I remember watching one man carving a pair of wooden wheels with a big butcher knife. All of us were worried sick, and many lined up at the latrines in their nervous need to urinate. Harold Decker was faithfully monitoring the BBC and Radio Luxembourg on our precious secret radio. The night before the move, he heard and copied down in shorthand an official announcement that an agreement had just been reached, through the Swiss Protecting Power, between the Allies and the Germans. No more prisoners were to be moved either out of Europe by us or into the Alpine Redoubt by the Germans. The next day when we were ordered to line up at the gate for departure, we refused to go and pointed out that this new agreement had been reached. The Germans checked and found this to be correct, and the order was countermanded, thank God.

Sometime in March, I came down with pneumonia again and was given a bunk in the lazarette, which was nothing more than a room with double bunks and a little extra space. An American prisoner-doctor and a few noble *kriegies* were doing the chores so we could stay in bed and recover. I don't remember how long I stayed there, but with some sulfa drugs, warmth, a special food ration, and rest, I recovered fairly promptly. The weather was wet but warming up, so we no longer suffered from the cold.

Most of the hot food that we prepared for ourselves had to be cooked outside. The small coal stoves in each block were totally inadequate for the numbers of *kriegies* now stuffed into this camp. It wasn't long before men started making ingenious little blast furnaces out of tin cans. They were mounted on boards and consisted of a small blower spun by a crank and connected to a little

One of our many little tin stoves in action. Army Signal Corps photograph, courtesy of the Air Force Academy Library

tin stove on which a small pot could be placed. A fire made of cardboard, wood chips, and small pieces of wood would boil water and cook food when kept burning hard by the air forced under it from the blower. It was a two-man operation, and almost every mess group or syndicate had one of these stoves. The smoke from hundreds of them hung over the camp all day long. The demand for wood to feed these stoves soon resulted in the gradual but steady destruction of the flooring, walls, and partitions in the barracks. The goons found it impossible to stop this practice. In the past they would have taken aggressive action, but their control was visibly weakening.

On every clear day we were presented with an impressive display of American air power. We watched most of it from the slit trenches into which we were ordered as soon as the sirens announced an approaching raid. Most of the raids were on Munich, and the bombers were clearly visible as they passed across our southern sky. The stream of airplanes seemed endless, and we were often in the slit trenches all day long with never a moment when the bombers were out of sight. We saw no fighter action, although there probably was some. On occasion, after the all-clear sounded, several of the beautiful Luftwaffe ME-262 jet fighters flew over us at rooftop height at very high speed, and their roar sounded like a bomb going off. They raised the shingles on the roofs of our huts. We loved it, and a great cheer would go up. These pilots knew who we were, and I guess it was good for their morale even this late in the war to see how many of us they had actually taken out of the war. They were flying against hopeless odds and facing an inevitable and imminent defeat.

In early April we began to worry about the possibility of serious disorder in the camp as the war grew nearer daily. There was no way to predict how the Germans would handle the surrender of this huge mass of hostile men of various Allied nations. Nor could

Davy Jones and the Americans who worked with him on the tunnels at Stalag Luft III. From left to right: Jim Cleary, Dave Brown, Bert Wiel, Goss, Jones, Buck Inghram, Anderson, Schierly. Photograph from the Air Force Academy Library was taken discreetly by clandestine camera at Stammlager VIIA for the historical record.

Francis Finnegan and his code workers at Stalag Luft III. From left to right: front row—Draper, Cleary, Oberg; next row—Stine, Finnegan, Boyle; farther back between Draper and Finnegan is Embach; in top row between Boyle and Oberg is Eldridge. Unfortunately, the others are unidentified. Photograph from the Air Force Academy Library was taken discreetly at Stammlager VIIA for the historical record.

we be sure that, at the last minute, the SS or Gestapo would not undertake to vent their spleen in a rampage at our expense.

We knew we could control our officers, but the 10,000 to 20,000 enlisted men of several different nations—the United States, England, France, Italy, Russia, and others—worried us. There was little real leadership in their camps, and they all worked hard all day every day, mostly in bomb damage clearance in Munich. They marched out at daybreak, were taken by train to Munich, and returned at dusk, dirty, hungry, and apathetic. They had no leisure time and were a scruffy looking bunch. Their leaders were called Men of Confidence, and they had been selected by vote from among their peers. The men had no real authority except through personal leadership, yet some of them were truly outstanding. We called for volunteers from among some of our best officers to swap identities with some of the enlisted men so they could get into the enlisted camps and provide some leadership in the event of trouble. We had no difficulty talking some enlisted men into switching, since they regarded the officer lifestyle as very desirable.

I have always regretted that we were unable to obtain recognition after the war for the officers who volunteered to switch camps. They made a real sacrifice in our overall best interests by agreeing to go over the fence into a crowded and dirty environment. Had there been a serious situation, they were prepared to try to organize the enlisted men. Fortunately, we never had to call on them.

On about 6 April, Col. Paul V. Goode arrived on foot with about 1,000 army officers from the unfortunate camp at Hammelsberg. The Hammelsberg story is an extraordinary one. Its prisoners had originally been confined in Oflag 64 at Shubin in Poland and had been evacuated and marched west on 21 January 1945, just a

Col. Paul V. Goode, second from left, and three of his staff at Oflag 64, Shubin, Poland, with a visitor from the Swiss Protecting Power, center. On the far left is Lt. Col. John K. Waters. Courtesy of the Air Force Academy Library

few days before our march started, to prevent them from being liberated by the rapidly advancing Russians. "Pop" Goode was their SAO. He was a member of the West Point class of 1917 and had been captured at Normandy. Everywhere he went as a prisoner he became the SAO because of his age and seniority. He had been through the mill too—captured in heavy fighting and bombed at the POW camp at Limberg with loss of some seventeen men. When his 1,471 U.S. Army officers and enlisted men were evacuated from Shubin, they were marched 345 miles across Germany in the dreadful winter weather to an old camp at Hammelsberg holding Serbian prisoners. That small town was about seventy miles east of Frankfurt on the Main. It took them forty-five days, and they arrived with only 423 men. Most of the losses along the way were due to escapes, sickness, exhaustion, and frostbite.

Goode's next most senior officer was Lt. Col. John K. Waters, West Point class of 1931. He had been captured at Kasserine Pass, Algeria, in February 1943. John's wife, Beatrice, was Gen. George Patton's daughter. At this time (late February and early March 1945), General Patton's army was holding the line through Frankfurt, and it is widely believed that the Red Cross had informed Patton that Waters, along with some 500 of his colleagues from Shubin, were now at this camp just seventy miles beyond his front lines.

Patton then made one of his worst mistakes of the war. He ordered a small task force to be inserted through the German lines at night to race to Hammelsberg, liberate the camp, and bring out the American prisoners. It turned into a disaster. John Waters was shot and seriously wounded in an attempt, under a white flag, to negotiate the surrender of the camp. The task force tried amid chaos to make a quick turnaround and move out with as many *kriegies* as they could carry, and it was ambushed and quickly destroyed only a few miles from the camp. Only a handful of men avoided being killed, wounded, or captured and got back through the lines. The Germans moved the Americans out of the camp the next day, and they were marched, under Goode's leadership, down to Bavaria where they joined us.

Goode became the SAO in our huge camp. Waters was left behind in the care of a Serbian prisoner-doctor who kept him alive until Patton's main forces overran the camp about a week later. Waters survived and went on to serve as a distinguished four-star army general. Goode, as a captain, had been a tactical officer at West Point when I was a cadet in the 1930s. He was one of the few such officers whom cadets held in high regard. He could be tough in disciplinary matters, but he was fair and had a wonderful sense of humor. He immediately placed me on his staff as his A-2, in charge of intelligence and clandestine operations—the same job Waters had held on Goode's staff until the disaster.

By this time most of us were content to sit tight and await liberation by the advancing American forces. A few men still wanted to take their chances and go out. The favored plan was to sneak out of our compound and join the enlisted troops as they marched off to work in Munich. Escaping from the work groups in Munich would be relatively easy, as the enlisted men rarely tried to escape and were loosely guarded. John Lewis was one who wanted to go out this way. John was an eager escapee and had been out before and recaptured. Shot down in North Africa, he evaded the enemy for days in the desert before being turned in to the Germans by the Arabs. The Arabs were everywhere and in the pay of the Germans.

The gate to our compound was locked with a big old-fashioned brass padlock. Its key, which hung on the belt of our *Lager* NCO, was rather complicated, with a center hole that went over a pin in the keyhole of the lock. Our con men worked hard on this particular goon with conversation, coffee, and chocolate until he was quite tame, and one day during an animated discussion, we made an impression of his key in soft soap without removing it from his belt. One of our skilled handymen, Charlie Hupert, then made a duplicate key. We would have no chance to test it. It had to work the first time it was used. The key had a short stem and would have to be turned with a pair of pliers, so, on the planned day and time, with the enlisted men marching past, John and I went out a window and I opened the gate to let him out. The key worked perfectly, and I didn't see John again for years. He managed to get away and was eventually overrun by our advancing forces in the Brenner Pass. He made it home well before the rest of us.

Looking back over our thirty-three months of escape efforts, I could count only six South Campers who reached friendly hands. Many more tried, but the odds of getting out of Germany undetected were extremely poor. The six who made it were Lt. Wesley Bedrick and Lt. Alvin "Sam" Vogle; Tony Alaimo, Shorty Spire, and John Lewis, who, as I remember, all went out at Moosburg; and Maj. Jerry Sage, who made his escape after he left Stalag Luft III and joined his army colleagues at Oflag 64. In due course, Hal Decker had received a message over his secret radio saying, "Sam and Shorty arrived okay."

On 13 April, we received word that President Roosevelt had died. I think the Germans took this news more seriously than we did. We all knew that the president had been in poor health for a long time. The Germans, on the other hand, were used to a one-man authoritarian form of government and may have thought our president's death might somehow change the course of the war. The news caused hardly a ripple amongst us, for we knew that the war would proceed vigorously until the end without change of strategy. On 30 April, only about two weeks later, Hitler killed himself, to our great relief. We still lived in the shadow of the Gestapo and the SS troops, but the threat of Alpine Redoubt faded away.

By mid-April the rigorous German security began to loosen, and I obtained a forged pass that allowed me to go out to the parcel warehouse near town. I was stunned to see the mountainous stacks of Red Cross food parcels, and came to understand what a

Tents were set up to handle the overflow of new kriegies. *Courtesy of the Air Force Academy Library*

huge and demanding job it was to feed the almost 100,000 prisoners who now depended largely on this source of food.

Tents had been set up in camp to handle the overflow of prisoners who continued to come in from the north. Among these new arrivals, many of whom came in groups that had walked long distances, were our people from the Center and West Camps who had been sent to Nuremberg while we were on the march. They had been on the road for several weeks and had been living off the land to a great extent. They were in better shape than we were. The latrines began to overflow, as the pump trucks that pumped them out daily were unable to keep up with the demand. Soon this filth was oozing everywhere, even into the tents where many men were now sleeping on the ground.

About this time I witnessed a remarkable example of British army bonding between officers and their other ranks. The personnel in British army units were not shifted around, so they stayed together for years. Yet the officers from the regiments captured during the Battle of France in the summer of 1940 had been immediately separated from their men. The men went to labor camps in the Sudeten Lands, and many dug coal for the next four years. In early April some of these men arrived in our camp. They were in dreadful condition, having marched for months from the Sudeten Lands under very difficult conditions. I saw their guards beating them as they came in. They passed by a camp of British army officers and suddenly, when it became apparent that they were from the same regiment, many happy shouts of recognition were passed through the wire. They hadn't seen each other since the British disaster at Dunkirk. The men were placed for the night in an open *Lager* and bedded down on the ground. When I saw them the next morning, they were clean-shaven with boots and brass shined, and they looked quite presentable. The Germans were surprised when they saw this and regarded it as a threat to the security of the camp. They immediately marched these men out of the camp to a different location.

I saw some interesting and tragic events as I wandered around outside the camp using my fake pass. Once, I saw a truckload of concentration camp prisoners parked at our front gate. The driver had stopped to obtain food and water for these poor wretches. Wearing dirty striped suits, they were skin and bones, and their heads had been shaved. They clamored and fought each other for the food and water. Their deprivations had just about reduced them to the level of animals.

Another time, I tested my newfound freedom to the limit. I dressed in my leather flight jacket and uniform cap, wandered down into Moosburg, and sat down on the curb to watch what went by on the main street through town. Everything seemed to be going south. I remember a pathetic group of about four Hungarian soldiers (German allies) pushing a small artillery piece down the road. I also saw a big, burly, red-faced German in *Lederhosen* (short leather pants). He winked at me as he passed, walking south. A senior German army officer in a small sports car, accompanied by another officer, pulled up to the curb near me and studied his maps—probably for the forthcoming defense of the town. They paid no attention to me. What a strange and exciting experience it was, after being locked up for almost three years, to be able to sit on the curb in a small German town and watch as the war drew inexorably to its end.

Patton's army was getting very close, and we were seeing more and more U.S. aircraft—fighters and light bombers—passing nearby. Our radio made it clear that something would happen soon. One day an army lieutenant colonel (nonpilot) came in. He had just been captured riding around in a Jeep. He announced that he was a staff officer in the headquarters that was planning our evacuation. He showed us a form that we were all required to fill out, and he said the oldest prisoners would go home first. To my great disappointment, however, none of his promises were fulfilled.

Finally, on the evening of 28 April, Pop Goode told me to join him for a meeting with the German camp commandant, the old Stalag Luft III vice commandant, Major Zimoliet, and his staff. Also present were Lt. Col. Dick Klocko, RAF Group Captain Willetts, and several of his staff. In a very businesslike manner, plans were made for an orderly turnover, on the morrow, of control of Stammlager VIIA from the Germans to the senior American and British officer prisoners and, of course, to the oncoming American forces, which were expected to move through during the morning with little resistance. Dick Klocko and a British wing commander were directed to go into town immediately and establish liaison with the mayor and maintain communications between the town and our leaders until told to stand down.

Years later, Dick Klocko told a wonderful story about that first night in town. He said the mayor put the two of them up in a nice inn. Dick was given the bridal suite, and his British colleague was given the next room. Dick said he chuckled when he noticed that, when retiring to his room, the Brit put his muddy boots in the hall to be shined, as is customary in Europe. Dick thought to himself that no one but a Brit, in the chaos at the end of a total war, would do such a silly thing, but the next morning the boots were shined.

Pop Goode, Group Captain Kellett, and several others then departed before midnight to make contact with the German sector defense commander. Pop and his party spent the night traveling under a white flag to and from the command post of the U.S. 14th Armored Division, conveying a German proposal to establish the area around the POW camp as neutral ground. The commander of the 14th rejected the proposal, fed the party a good breakfast, and then sent them back with instructions to keep their heads down in the morning, as the division would come through at about nine o'clock with only minor rearguard resistance from the Germans.

When Pop Goode got back I joined him and the rest of his staff in his room, and he told us of his interesting night. He pulled a piece of white bread out of his pocket. It looked to us like cake. He quietly mentioned that he had eaten bacon and eggs for breakfast. About that time the Germans blew up the two local bridges over the Iser River that ran north and south in front of the camp, and the shooting started. Most of it was small-arms fire over the camp. We then heard a prolonged, loud "thump" as 100,000 kriegies hit the floor.

I had directed John Bennett and Dick Schrupp, both accomplished photographers, to get out front early and photograph everything. I damned near got them killed. They watched the SS tanks and panzer foust grenadiers (antitank bazooka soldiers) take their positions, and they also watched the approach of our tanks. When the shooting started, they dove into a trench and found themselves with a bunch of local goons who were as scared as they were. They finally made their way back to safety and returned, after the shooting stopped, to take the wonderful pictures that we still treasure of the first U.S. tank to enter the camp, the surrender of the German commandant, and the raising of the American flag over the camp.

The excitement in camp was indescribable. As soon as the shooting stopped, men started popping up by the thousands all over camp. They climbed up on the roofs of the huts and even on the wire to get a view of what was going on. When they spotted an

All of these kriegies *are smiling as they surround a GI soldier who came into our camp as a liberator immediately after the surrender. He is in the middle of the crowd holding his Browning automatic rifle over his head.*

Kriegies *emerging as the shooting stopped. Photo taken with a clandestine camera*

American flag going up on one of the more prominent buildings in Moosburg, they knew for sure that the war was over for us. Men were hugging each other, crying, praying, screaming, and jumping up and down. Everyone rushed out of the huts, and the crowd grew so large that each man had to do his celebrating in place. The roar was impressive, and the whole scene was very moving.

This flag at the front gate had just been raised. Photo by Dick Schrupp taken with one of our clandestine cameras

I went out front as soon as the shooting stopped and watched the German garrison personnel come into the commandant's headquarters. First the officers disarmed themselves and dumped their weapons in a pile. These officers were soon trucked away without ceremony. Then the

Front gate of Stammlager VIIA after the liberation. Photograph from the Air Force Academy Library

The actual surrender at Stammlager VIIA. From left to right: Maj. Gustov Simoleit, the Stammlager VIIA commandant; Lt. Col. James W. Lann, the commander of the 47th Tank Battalion, the unit that liberated the camp; and Group Captain Willett, RAF, the senior British officer and senior Allied POW. Photo taken by John Bennett with one of our clandestine cameras

soldiers began to arrive. It took some time to bring them all in from their posts around the large camp. They were loaded into trucks, standing up and crammed in tightly. When the drivers thought the trucks were full, they would lurch forward then brake sharply and crowd in more German soldiers. Those men were treated with brazen hostility, and we had our first taste of the hatred toward the Germans that a long and bitter war had generated. We prisoners had been accommodating for so long in order to survive. The sight of this grim callousness was a shock to me when I first saw it.

One German SS soldier was brought in on a litter to our front gate. He was unconscious and bleeding from his mouth and ears, probably the result of a severe head injury. There was an argument about whether to admit him to our POW hospital, and I suspect he was simply allowed to die. There were other bodies of German soldiers visible up in the hills to the west of camp where the young, largely untrained soldiers had been given their choice of being shot for dereliction of duty or of manning a panzer foust in a foxhole to stop the oncoming American tanks. I understood that one tank was in fact disabled with loss of life just as it approached the camp.

Moose Stillman gathered up five or six of the German officers' ceremonial daggers from the pile of surrendered arms and gave one to me. Moose, Dick Schrupp, and I climbed on a tank and rode gloriously around outside the camp. I felt intoxicated with joy at finally being free. I noticed sandbags placed around the turrets of the tanks to increase their resistance to penetration of enemy anti-tank projectiles. Many also were cluttered with the booty "liberated" in the towns they had come through. There were bolts of silk, fur coats, antique arms, beautiful quilts—the spoils of war. I was disappointed to see this.

R. E. Williams, an old *kriegie* and fighter pilot who had moved clandestine parcels into South Camp, told us he had seen Sergeant

Me, Stillman, and Schrupp on one of the first tanks to arrive at the camp. Photo by John Bennett with one of our clandestine cameras

Glemnitz in the back of a truck about to be driven off to POW camp. Glemnitz had said in a voice filled with agony and despair, "Mr. Villiams, Germany has lost another vah, vat am I going to do? Vat am I to do?" What he did was most remarkable. I learned about it when I went to Berlin thirty-some years later to get his oral history. His family (a wife and two young daughters), when last he knew, was in Breslau, which fell to the Russians after heavy fighting in late April 1945. Glemnitz stuck with his duty to the bitter end, but he did not remain a prisoner long. He was able to talk his way out of the miserable, unsheltered fields in which the thousands of Germans were being held. Men with building and repair skills were being released to help get vital utilities and services going again. Glemnitz put a pack on his back and, with incredible luck and persistence, made his way through the Russian lines to Breslau, found his family, and brought them out to the British sector of Berlin.

A lot of Russians were being held in the camp, but they were fairly well isolated from us the whole time we were there. They were miserably treated and were very hungry. They had been at the bottom of the German spectrum of treatment of prisoners. It's hard to grasp what that meant, but we now know that of the 3 million Russian prisoners captured by the Germans during the war, 2 million died of neglect. They were starved, died of exposure in the winter, and received no medical attention. One night, soon after we arrived in the camp and were on very short rations ourselves, a German NCO brought a Russian of unknown rank to see Rojo Goodrich. The Russian wanted us to share our Red Cross parcels with them. Rojo told the Russian that we could not do it and that was the end of that. We had been told that the International Red Cross had offered to feed the Russian prisoners but that Stalin declined the offer on the grounds that the Red Cross was primarily an espionage organization.

We did not know it, and I suppose the Germans didn't either, but there were about ten Russian generals among those Russian

The Russian generals, newly liberated POWs, at Stammlager VIIA. Photo taken with one of our clandestine cameras

prisoners at Stammlager VIIA. As soon as they were free, they all dressed up in their proper clothes and we took a group photo of them. A few days later, big black limousines arrived and took them all away. God only knows where they were taken, but I know that General Eisenhower, under instructions from Roosevelt and Churchill, sent all of the Russian ex-prisoners back to Russia at Stalin's request. Most had to be forced to go, and Solzhenitsyn tells us in his *Gulag Archipelago* that the officers were shot and the enlisted men all went to the gulags. Stalin is reported to have said that if they survived the war in captivity, they must have collaborated. As soon as the local Russians were liberated, they went on a rampage and terrorized the poor, helpless German civilians in and around Moosburg. There were many rapes and lots of drunkenness, and private homes were invaded and ransacked for food.

I immediately moved out of the room where I had been sleeping on a table to avoid the bedbugs, and I found a cot in one of the nice, clean German offices in the *Vorlager*. I explored the whole

German administrative area and found the card files on which the goons meticulously kept our personal POW history. These cards had our photo along with place and date of capture, injuries and wounds, hospitalizations, escape attempts, punishments, and so on. I sent them into camp, and they were distributed to all as a coveted keepsake. I also ran across a large chest. It must have been three feet high and about three by four feet square. I opened it and found that it was full of U.S. money. I figured it was the money that the Germans had confiscated from the *kriegies* over the years. I don't have any idea what became of that money when our troops took over the camp a few chaotic days later.

On the night of 3 May Lieutenant Colonel Earp of 3rd Army Headquarters assumed command of the camp from Group Captain Willetts, RAF, who, as a former POW, had been the senior Allied officer. Earp commanded an artillery battalion that had been pulled out of the line to service the camp and the many other *kriegies* bivouacking in the vicinity.

The afternoon we were liberated I found my West Point classmate Bill Connor looking for me. We had gone to prep school together before entering the academy, and he was a distinguished graduate. He commanded a "flash-and-sound" battalion near the front lines in the 14th Armored Division. His unit used special instruments to quickly locate enemy artillery by the flash and the sound of the firing. Knowing the location, they were able to immediately direct the division's counter-battery fire. Bill took me to his headquarters, which was located in a beautiful old estate in a nearby forest. His people probably gave the owners fifteen minutes to get out. I got a hot bath, a change of underwear, some good chow, and a good night's sleep in a real bed with clean sheets. I told Bill I wanted a German helmet and rifle to bring home to my son. My father had brought me the same two souvenirs when he came home from France in 1919. Bill found these items for me in a few minutes. I still have parts of the rifle my father brought me, and my son, Pat, still has the rifle and helmet that I brought him.

General Patton, commander of the 3rd Army, pays us a visit two or three days after we were liberated. Photo taken with one of our clandestine cameras

The day after we were liberated, Colonel Horner, the G-2 of III Corps, 3rd Army, looked me up, and I told him all I knew about the various anti-Nazi resistance groups that were forming in the rear of the retreating Germans. One rather formidable group was trying to take over Munich and wanted us to join them. We wanted no part of it. I spent several interesting days with Colonel Horner and his staff. They took me along when they moved forward following the advance of the corps, and I stayed with them overnight in a small village, sleeping in a family dwelling also abruptly requisitioned. It was very comfortable.

About two days after we were liberated, General Patton paid us a visit. He came into the camp standing in his Jeep, wearing his helmet, and girded with his ivory-handled revolvers. He dismounted, waded into the mass of *kriegies* gathered around him, and poked his head into one of the filthy blocks. What he said is lost to history, but it was probably typical Patton. I do not believe that Colonel Goode bothered to meet with him.

When I returned to the camp, I found that the Red Cross had established Moosburg as a regional distribution center for food parcels. For some time, even before the end of hostilities, the Red Cross had been delivering food to groups of prisoners on the roads and in bivouac camps over a wide area, using a fleet of white trucks driven by Canadian POWs. Many of the groups they helped had been starving.

The local artillery battalion had a big job just to feed us and empty the latrines. Their commander ordered us to stay put and promised early evacuation. This was too much for many of the men to take, and they started trickling out and heading for Paris on their own. I've heard some marvelous accounts of the adventures experienced by these men as they hitchhiked to Paris.

We soon learned that General DeGaulle had prevailed upon General Eisenhower to give first priority to the evacuation of all French prisoners. Since there were several thousand of them out on farms in Bavaria (managed out of Stammlager VIIA), they all had to be brought in, processed, and airlifted back to France. I was impressed by the efficiency of the French prisoner administrative staff that handled this job. The first thing I noticed was that a large German office building in the *Vorlager* had been taken over by the French, and it was filled with men typing up records for all the French prisoners. They had commandeered every typewriter in the German garrison offices and were quietly preparing the necessary forms and records for thousands of prisoners, most of whom had been in Germany since the fall of France in 1940. We waited an agonizing week for them to be evacuated.

The war was over, so there was little for me to do. I longed to head home. Pop Goode had organized all of the Americans into companies, each with a strong commander, and they were ready to move out on a moment's notice. It was a heartbreaking sight for me and several other fairly senior officers who were old prisoners when Jeeps started coming in to pick up almost all of our full colonels. Apparently on General Spaatz's orders, they were taken to his headquarters back in France. Most of them had not been prisoners for long. We old prisoners felt like we'd been forgotten.

We watched Rojo Goodrich, Lou Parker, Joe Miller, Jake Smart, A. Y. Smith, Bill Kennedy, Moose Stillman, C. D. Jones, and several others drive out the gate stuffed into Jeeps and waving good-bye. We bitterly recalled the assurances of that staff weenie who had joined us shortly before the end. He had assured us that the oldest prisoners would go home first. Maj. Davy Jones and I agreed, in an emotional pique, that we would stay until the end and close the gate behind us. The thousands of junior officers and enlisted men were still there, and most of the senior leadership left them without a concern. Col. Pop Goode and his company commanders, however, stayed.

Willie Lanford had a visitor from his old bomb group who brought him some food and clothing. Willie gave this officer my big cardboard box of scrapbooks with instructions to send it to Lt. Col. A. P. Clark, 215 Young Street, San Antonio, Texas. It was there waiting for me when I got home. I sent Willie a check for seventy-five dollars, as that was what a case of Scotch cost at that time, if you could get it, which was almost impossible.

There was one more thing I wanted to do before we left the area, and that was to go see the German ME-262 jet fighter. We were not too far from the German air depot base near Erding. Dick Schrupp and I borrowed a Jeep and, with one or two others, went down to this old permanent prewar base. There were signs of bomb damage. Various aircraft, all in unflyable condition, were scattered around the field. As a final gesture before abandoning their aircraft, the departing pilots had detonated hand grenades in some the cockpits.

I was thrilled to see that there were two or three hangars full of ME-262s. Most appeared to have been in for engine changes, and we had a good look at them and brought home some pictures. They were truly beautiful aircraft. Their jet engines placed them well ahead of the leading edge of aircraft design anywhere else in the world. If they had entered the war as fighters earlier, they would have made a great difference in the air war. There was not much of anything else left in the depot. We found many parachutes, but all had had their "throats cut" and the silk was gone. Many people had already been through the place in the few days since the war ended, and they had looted whatever they wanted.

One of the ME-262s at Erding Air Base. I photographed this with one of our clandestine cameras

CHAPTER 11

Going Home

10 May to 26 May 1945

Finally, on about 10 May, my turn came. I departed the wretched, filthy camp, following the group that Davy commanded, and closed the gate behind me. All the Stalag Luft III *kriegies* were gone. There were still prisoners of other nations and, I believe, some British colonial troops in the camp. I don't know how they finally got home. We climbed into heavy trucks and were taken to one of several nearby German secondary airfields, which included the ones at Landshut and Straubing. From there we were to be air-evacuated in C-47 Gooney Birds to the huge replacement depots on the French coast. The one that we would all be crowded into was just north of the port of Le Havre, named Camp Lucky Strike.

A crowd of kriegies *arriving by truck on the field at Landshut. Photo taken with one of our clandestine cameras*

Kriegies *enplaning at Landshut for Camp Lucky Strike. Photo taken with one of our clandestine cameras*

I arrived at Landshut to see another chaotic scene. Many of the *kriegies* who had departed Moosburg several days before were still there waiting, without shelter or any amenities, for an aircraft to take them out. Dozens of C-47s were parked on the field and others were circling, waiting for room to land. The field was a small grass runway marked only by white wooden blocks and badly cut up by deep ruts. When I arrived, an aircraft was burning at one end of the field. It had ground-looped on landing and collided with another parked aircraft. I was told that the copilot had been killed. It was clear to me that the runway needed to be moved and, there being no one else to do it, I took it upon myself, with Dick Schrupp's help, to go out and move the marker blocks to an area that had not been torn up.

A small medical evacuation hospital was located on the edge of the field, but there were no hangars. The field had obviously been occupied by an army medical unit to air-evacuate combat casualties but, of course, there were none now. Much confusion prevailed, and some of our people lost their luggage. Many army stevedore troops and former Russian prisoners roamed around on the field at will, and the Russians "liberated" everything they could get their hands on. I was appalled when I discover that there was no airport authority and no radio control of the aircraft landing and taking off. About the second day I was there, an armored reconnaissance battalion arrived and proceeded to establish order. I checked in with the commander and found that he was Maj. George W. England, a West Pointer, class of 1939. He wasted no time getting the people who had no business there off the field. After announcing his orders to that effect, he put tanks at opposite corners of the field and fired a few bursts of machine gun fire into the air, clearing the field.

George England was very kind to me and invited me to stay with him until my time came to depart. His staff had found a house up on a hill in a suburb overlooking the town. I suppose the owners had been given the usual short notice to get out. It was a very fine house of some five or six bedrooms, and was built in a square with the rooms around a center parlor that was open up to the roof. I ate and slept in luxury. I remember that I could see the distant railroad marshaling yards from the house, and I noted that they were completely torn up from heavy bombing.

The next day, a German aircraft came in and landed on the field. It was a small twin-engine passenger plane, and as it approached to land, it was shot at and missed by the antiaircraft unit "protecting" the field. After it landed, the pilot simply cut his engines and sat there. I'm sure he was glad to be alive and in the hands of Americans instead of the Russians. I borrowed a pistol from an officer of England's staff, jumped into a "follow me" Jeep flying a big yellow flag, and roared out to accept the surrender of these Germans. I directed the pilot to clear the runway, but he was unable to get both engines restarted, so we had the crew and passengers disembark there. An ambulance came out to take the prisoners away, and a large crowd gathered, which included trophy hunters who sought to strip the decorations off the uniformed crew and passengers. I protested, as I knew that under the Geneva Convention they were authorized to keep their decorations.

Eventually we towed the aircraft off the field, and it was immediately commandeered by some army general's aide who intended to save it for his personal use. I had a chance to rummage through the aircraft before it disappeared, and I acquired a pistol and a pair of binoculars, which I still have. We learned that German aircraft were coming in to surrender at many airfields held by Americans. They all came from behind the Russian lines and were content to be in our custody, although some aircraft had women and children on board, many of whom were very roughly handled by unruly crowds and stripped of all of their valuables upon landing.

I was having a ball in the leadership role I had assumed and was oblivious to the fact that I was operating without any real authority. I guess I was so used to being a senior officer in a camp full of lieutenants and captains that I was acting as if nothing had changed. I was about to find out how far off base I was.

That same afternoon a C-47 towing a big glider appeared over the field. The glider cut loose, circled, and landed. I went over to see who they were. To my joy and relief I found that the crew was an airport traffic control unit with equipment to handle landing and departing aircraft. I told them how welcome they were and started to brief them on the problems we'd been experiencing. They didn't seem very interested and were preoccupied backing a camouflaged army sedan out of the glider. They hadn't yet started unpacking their huge boxes of radios and other equipment. As they all jumped into the car, I asked them where they were going. They replied that they were going to find suitable billets. I was astonished. The chaotic aircraft traffic situation was obviously in need of immediate attention. These new arrivals just drove off, quite unconcerned about the situation. Later, when they returned, I was again hanging over them, trying to get them into action. Finally, the captain in charge turned to me and said, "Colonel, we have secret equipment here and we have been sent by General Norstad to do this job. If you don't bug

I am standing in line for a free issue, probably a toothbrush. Photographed with one of our clandestine cameras

off and leave us alone, I am going to have to report you to the general." That brought me down to earth in a hurry. I immediately "bugged off," traipsing across the field to get in line with my fellow *kriegies*. Shortly thereafter I boarded an airplane and departed for Camp Lucky Strike. That was about 14 May.

The five-hour flight was extremely interesting, as I could see the devastation of German towns and cities below us. The pilot of the airplane was a lieutenant colonel whom I had known before, and he invited me up to the cockpit and let me fly for about an hour. This hour turned out to be of crucial importance later in establishing eligibility for continuing my flying status through my thirty-three months of captivity. I later learned that we were being given lots of breaks concerning our flight status and other matters, and being eligible for flying pay while a prisoner was one of them.

Camp Lucky Strike was one of three huge replacement depots, now empty, through which the thousands of soldiers sent over to replace losses had been fed into the divisions in combat. They all had cigarette names—Camp Camel, Lucky Strike, and, I guess, Philip Morris as well. Lucky Strike had pyramidal tents as far as the eye could see. So many POW camps had been liberated ahead of schedule that it was full to overflowing. I was in a tent with about six others from Stalag Luft III but no one I had known before. Our tent had iron cots, but they had no mattresses, and, of course, we had a dirt floor. The food lines were so long that one was lucky to get one meal a day for the first few days that I was there. German prisoners were doing the KP work, and they were very happy to be there, as we were being fed an especially rich ration of which they probably got their share. We were issued new uniforms—Eisenhower jackets and matching trousers plus all the other necessary clothing, toilet articles, and insignia that we needed. There was a medical clinic for those in need, and we all drew partial pay.

The second day I was there, I was standing in the main camp street among literally thousands of other kriegies when I spotted Lt. Col. Henry Katz approaching. He'd been my West Point roommate, and he was looking for me, but could have looked for days if

A typical crowd in the street at Camp Lucky Strike. Photo taken with one of our clandestine cameras

he hadn't just run into me by luck. He had a bottle of the famous B&B brandy made by the monks at Fécamp, a little town nearby. We had a nice visit, and I planned to take the brandy home as a fine souvenir, but that was not to be. After several more frustrating days, I knocked the neck off the bottle and shared it with my tentmates.

I had been very disappointed to learn that the intelligence people in Washington, with whom we had been working, had tried to search out from among the *kriegies* flowing out of Stammlager VIIA the key people in our clandestine operations. As these men came through Lucky Strike, they had been pulled out of the line and were promptly flown back to Washington. I found that most of my people had gone home this way. By the time I got into the system, the intel people felt that they had enough of the key people and showed no interest in me. There I was, the second oldest American service *kriegie* in the theater and the officer in charge of escape and other clandestine activities in the oldest camp. No one was even interested in getting a report from me, and they had flown some of my least important workers home ahead of me. Needless to say, I was more than a little annoyed.

After a few more days I couldn't stand it any longer, and I went to the tent of the most senior Lucky Strike staff officer I could find. I think he was a major. I unloaded my frustration, disappointment, and emotional distress on him. He heard me out and told me he was sending two officers to Paris in the morning with a Jeep and I could go with them. He gave me a written pass, the name of a hotel where I would be billeted, and he may have arranged for me to be flown home.

So the next morning, I climbed in with Capt. Cyrus Manierre, West Point class of 1942, who had been serving in the OSS when captured by the Gestapo. He had managed, as had Jerry Sage, to pose as an evading airman. His uncle was the U.S. ambassador to France. The other officer was a free French major who I think was also a count. He had been wounded and had high-level connections on General DeGaulle's staff.

The cathedral of Notre Dame in Rouen. I took this photo with one of our clandestine cameras.

I left camp Lucky Strike with no regrets and enjoyed our day-long ride to Paris. I had one of our clandestine cameras with me and took some photos along the way. We stopped for lunch in Rouen, and I saw the beautiful cathedral of Notre Dame de Rouen and the church of St. Ouen. Notre Dame had been badly battered but not destroyed by the bombing of the vital Rouen bridge across the Seine River. This bridge was a key target in cutting German communications in preparation for the invasion on 6 June 1944. The cathedral was less than a mile from the bridge, and nothing was left standing between it and the river where the bridge had been.

We arrived in Paris in the late afternoon and drove past L'Arc de Triomphe, from which were hanging the four huge flags of the Allies: Britain's, France's, ours, and that of the USSR. The latter huge, red flag dominated the scene. VE-Day was declared on 8 May, and we were entering Paris on about 16 May.

Somehow or other, Paris seemed to be filled with my buddies from South Camp, and together we did the things one should do in Paris. I went to the Follies and to Mass on Sunday at the cathedral of Notre Dame. My most memorable moment in Paris was kneeling quietly in the cathedral. I had an opportunity to pause in the hectic rush to get home and thank the good Lord for keeping me alive through my long captivity. I rode the metro and tried to buy some things for Carolyn and my two girls. Although there was little of value in the stores, I bought small dolls dressed as French peasants for my daughters. They still treasure these dolls almost sixty years later.

After a few days, I found myself on a C-54 bound for home. I say found myself, for I cannot remember how I managed to acquire a seat on that flight. In fact, it was a VIP flight returning distinguished newspaper people and journalists who had come over as guests of General Eisenhower to see the Nazi concentration camp horrors. Among them were Edna Ferber and Amen Carter, the distinguished owner and publisher of the Fort Worth newspaper. His

The soft focus from this shot, taken by me after D-Day with one of our clandestine cameras, doesn't capture the full poignancy of L' Arc de Triomphe in Paris and the four Allied flags.

son had been a *kriegie* with us but had already gone home. There were also several generals aboard, and one of them was kind enough to sign an authorization for me to take home the German rifle and pistol that I had carried with me from Moosburg and Landshut.

We landed the next day at Mitchel Field on Long Island to refuel. As I debarked, I saw Lieutenant Colonel Black standing at the foot of the ramp. He had been one of the last people I'd seen when we departed from Fort Hamilton by ship in May 1942. He wanted to know where I'd been the past three years, and he appeared incredulous when I told him that, except for a few days, I'd spent the whole time in Germany. I was asked to pose with him drinking a glass of milk. I should have asked him for the location of the nearest telephone so I could call Carolyn. I was in such a euphoric state, though, that I never even thought of it. I think I was also in a daze after all the emotional ups and downs of the previous three weeks.

We went on to Washington, and I was required to stay for three or four long days before I was free to go home. I stayed with my sister, Mary, and her husband, Lt. Col. Lawrence Lincoln. He and his big brother, Brig. Gen. George Arthur Lincoln, were assigned to General Marshall's staff in the Pentagon. I promptly checked in at the Pentagon intelligence office with which we had been working throughout the war. I dumped about two dozen undeveloped rolls of film on the desk of some colonel, but this generated none of the enthusiasm I had expected. In fact, the office personnel appeared to be closing down, as the war in Europe was over and perhaps their job was finished. Apparently a different office was working with the prisoners in the Pacific theater. I was not sure I would ever see the results of our priceless and dangerous photographic work. However, several months later I received a letter from a thoughtful colonel enclosing about seventy prints from our film. Over the years many copies have been made from these, and the original set is now part of the extensive Stalag

Having a cup of milk with Colonel Black at Mitchel Field.
Courtesy of Army Public Affairs

Luft III History Collection in the Air Force Academy Library. The
director of the office to which I reported insisted that I write a
report, which I did. After several days I was told I could go home.
I remember telling the Lincoln brothers that I believed Germany
was finished. I had no way of knowing then that President Truman
and General Marshall were soon to launch a massive effort to put
Germany back together.

Upon arrival in Washington, I was finally able to call Carolyn,
a great thrill for both of us. I'd practically forgotten the sound of
her voice. She told me that several of my colleagues who had
arrived in the States earlier had been kind enough to call her and

Carolyn and our children. This photo, taken in 1944, clearly shows the anxiety and worry that was part of their daily lives throughout the war.

tell her that I was on my way. Only later did I hear the full story of how she and the other *kriegie* families had managed to keep informed of our trek to Bavaria and our liberation by General Patton's army. In due course she had received a telegram from Washington advising her that on 29 April 1945 I had been "returned to military control." What a nice, official way to put it.

When I was finally released by the Pentagon, I hitched a ride on a flight to Atlanta. Marvin McNickle had arranged for me to accompany him on a C-45 that he was piloting. From Atlanta, I hitched a flight to Dallas. There being no flights available to San Antonio, I spent that Saturday night in the bachelor officers' quarters at Love Field. Early Sunday morning, I went down to flight operations and found no flights going to San Antonio or anywhere else. The place was like a tomb. This was about 26 May. I told the young captain on duty that I was a poor old former prisoner of war trying to get home, and he took pity on me. He set up a special flight for me in a Gooney Bird and off I went. The pilot let me fly a little, and, after landing at Kelly Field, I was met by an official car and driven straight home. By this time I had been free for almost one month. When I arrived at the house that Carolyn had bought and lived in for most of those previous three years, she and my three little children were standing on the front porch holding hands. I jumped from the car, shouldered my duffel bag, and ran across the yard through the lawn sprinkler. And then we all fell into each other's arms.

Bibliography

★ ★ ★

Brickhill, Paul. *The Great Escape.* London: Faber & Faber, 1953.

Burgess, Alan. *The Longest Tunnel: The True Story of World War II's Great Escape.* London: Bloomsbury Publishing, 1990.

Burton, Paul. *Escape From Terror.* Nederland, Tex.: Cate Media, 1995.

Chiesl, Oliver M. *Clipped Wings.* Seattle: Robert W. Kimball, 1948.

Constable, Trevor J. and Raymond F. Toliver. *Horrido!: Fighter Aces of the Luftwaffe.* London: Barker, 1968.

Diggs, Frank. *The Welcome Swede: The True Story of a Young Man Who Brought Hope to Thousands of Nazi Germany's Prisoners of War.* New York: Vantage Press, Inc., 1988.

Durand, Arthur. *Stalag Luft III: The Secret Story.* Baton Rouge: Louisiana State University Press, 1988.

Hehner, Barbara. *The Tunnel King: The True Story of Wally Floody and the Great Escape.* Toronto, Ont.: Harper-Collins, 2004.

McCright, Ewell Ross. *Behind the Wire: Stalag Luft III, South Compound.* Benton, Ark: Arnold A. Wright, 1993.

Parton, James. *"Air Force Spoken Here." General Ira Eaker and the Command of the Air.* Bethesda, Md.: Adler & Adler, 1986.

Sage, Col. Jerry. *Sage.* Wayne, Pa.: Miles Standish Press, 1985.

Smith, Sydney. *Wings Day: The Man Who Led the RAF's Epic Battle in German Captivity.* London: Collins, 1968.

Spivey, Delmar. *POW Odyssey: Recollections of Center Compound, Stalag Luft III, and the Secret German Peace Mission in World War II*. Attleboro, Mass.: Colonial Lithographics, Inc., 1964.

Toland, John. *The Last 100 Days: The Tumultuous and Controversial Story of the Final Days of World War II in Europe*. New York: Random House, 1966.

Toliver, Raymond T. and Hanns J. Scharff. *The Interrogator: The Story of Hans Scharff, Luftwaffe's Master Interrogator.* Fallbrook, Calif.: Aero Publishers, 1978.

Von Lindeiner-Wildau, Friedrich Wilhelm, Memoirs. Air Force Academy Library, Clark Special Collections Branch, Historical Collection of the Stalag Luft III Former Prisoners of War, Colorado Springs, CO.

Westheimer, David. *Sitting It Out: A World War II POW Memoir.* Houston: Rice University Press, 1992.

The Geneva Accords of 1929 and 1949.

The Department of Defense, *The Code of Conduct for The Military Man*, 1955.

Index

★ ★ ★

About the Author

★ ★ ★

Albert P. Clark was the sixth superintendent of the United States Air Force Academy, near Colorado Springs, Colorado. During his tenure as superintendent from August 1970 until July 1974, he was involved with all aspects of cadet life and instruction, as well as overseeing the operation of the academy.

Born at Schofield Barracks in Hawaii, he was raised in a military family. He graduated from the United States Military Academy, West Point, New York, in 1936 and completed flying training at Randolph Field in Texas in 1937. A command pilot, he is a graduate of the Armed Forces Staff College and the National War College.

In June 1942 General Clark went to England as second in command of the 31st Fighter Group, the first American fighter unit in the European theater of operations during World War II. He was shot down over Abbéville, France, in July 1942 and was held as a prisoner of war in Germany until April 1945.

He has held many key assignments, including time with Tactical Air Command, Continental Air Command, and Air Defense Command, prior to a tour of duty at Headquarters United States Air Force.

General Clark commanded the 48th Fighter Bomber Wing at Chaumont Air Base in France, 1955–1956, and then served as chief of staff of the United States Air Force in Europe (USAFE). He was director of military personnel at Headquarters USAF, 1959–1963, and then assigned to Okinawa as commander of the 313th Air Division.

In August 1965 he was named vice commander of the Tactical Air Command (TAC). He assumed duties as commander of Air University in August 1968. His military decorations include the Distinguished Service Medal with two oak leaf clusters, Legion of Merit with one oak leaf cluster, Air Medal, Air Force Commendation Medal, and the Purple Heart.

General Clark resides in Colorado Springs, Colorado.

Inside Military History
with Fulcrum Publishing

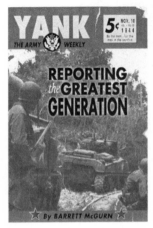

Yank: The Army Weekly
Reporting the Greatest Generation

Barrett McGurn
ISBN 1-55591-296-6 $18.95

Barrett McGurn has reminded us of the historic and valuable role played by YANK magazine as a freewheeling informational and morale-boosting tool in Word War II.

—Don Larrabee, retired Washington correspondent, former president of the National Press Club

☆ ☆ ☆ ☆ ☆

Falconry at the United States Air Force Academy
The Story of the Cadets' Unique Performing Mascot

A. P. Clark,
Lieutenant General, USAF (Ret.)
ISBN 1-55591-487-X (PB) $17.95
ISBN 1-55591-497-7 (HC) $34.95

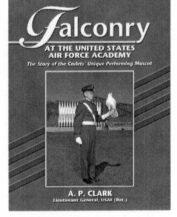

At the Academy, falcons are trained to fly free over stadiums filled with thousands of people and to perform thrilling aerial maneuvers—stoops and dives in recognizable simulation of the more spectacular aspects of the mission of the United States Air Force.

—from the Introduction

Fulcrum Publishing
16100 Table Mountain Parkway, Suite 300, Golden, CO 80403
To order call 800-992-2908 or visit www.fulcrum-books.com
Also available at your local bookstore.

Breinigsville, PA USA
30 March 2010
235231BV00001B/3/P